CW01305300

A GUARDSMAN'S LOT

BY

STEVE RUDGE

authorHOUSE™

1663 LIBERTY DRIVE, SUITE 200
BLOOMINGTON, INDIANA 47403
(800) 839-8640
WWW.AUTHORHOUSE.COM

This book is a work of non-fiction. Unless otherwise noted, the author and the publisher make no explicit guarantees as to the accuracy of the information contained in this book and in some cases, names of people and places have been altered to protect their privacy.

© 2005 STEVE RUDGE. All Rights Reserved.

No part of this book may be reproduced, stored in a retrieval system, or transmitted by any means without the written permission of the author.

First published by AuthorHouse 01/04/05

ISBN: 1-4208-2141-5 (sc)

*Printed in the United States of America
Bloomington, Indiana*

This book is printed on acid-free paper.

Dedications.

To Janice, for putting up with all the months of separation, that allowed me the time, to complete this manuscript.

Preface.

Steve Rudge served in the Grenadier Guards from 1966 to 1990, this is his story; from enlisting in the army as a boy soldier at only fifteen years old, to his subsequent retirement, as a Senior Warrant officer, having completed twenty five years Service.

This is a brutal interpretation of his life, with extremely strong language, and graphic detail.

It tells the reader about those twenty five years of his life through his eyes, described in a humorous manner, mixed with the reality of real people and the pitfalls that can be imposed by the inept and the arrogant when placed in a position of authority.

It shows how normal people placed in power are transformed into bullies and liars.

It shows how morality is at times forgotten by those whom should know better.

The book describes the camaraderie of men working under harsh conditions and the humour that evolves.

Notice:

The names have been changed and names have been omitted, mainly to protect the stupid. No offence was intended in the writing of this book it is an interpretation of my views and the views of others. If you are offended by what you read then you want to take a personality check and amend your views.

Chapter 1.
Hey "Fiddly De" "A Soldiers Life for me".

I stepped off the train at Brookwood in Surrey. Be there by fifteen thirty hours, May the 10th 1966, that was what the instructions read. Outside in the car park a green Bedford Army bus was collecting its cargo of wide eyed 15 year old apprehensive boys, such as myself.

"GET ON THE FUCKING BUS" the driver barked!

"I WANT MY FUCKING TEA," the driver again.

That sounded more like it. I had never really heard anyone swear in such graphic detail before, and the driver thought nothing of it. The closest that we ever came to hearing such language was when as stupid kids we were trying to be clever. Soon I would realise that this was going to teach me a whole New World, of the Queen's English. A Sergeant jumped up on the footplate and screamed

"SHUT FUCKING UP, THE LOT OF YOU, AND LISTEN".

What amazed me was that no one was talking, so why was he telling us to shut up? The world of the army was a strange place, still is I am sure.

"Right, listen in. This is the bus for the Guards Depot, Junior Guardsman Company. If you're not for it, fuck off now and get on the next train home. You may break your mother's heart but you're killing mine". Again the Sergeant is screaming.

A GUARDSMAN'S LOT

No one got off, too scared to, I think. Not wishing to loose face in front of all these new lads. The bus trundled on its route. This route, I can recollect as the longest two miles in my life, but we will come to that. The rest of the day was great, we were talked to, fed, and given a bed to sleep on, we were even permitted to go down to the NAAFI for some tea or a cold drinks. That was only after we had written a letter home telling all was fine. What did we know? At twenty two hundred hours (2200Hrs) we listened to a bugle playing some tune or other. Thereafter we were plunged into darkness, as someone shouted,

"lights out".

If you had been asleep prior to that, you would have been woken up by the volume of:

"LIGHTS OUT."

Strange place this army. In the dark interior of the barrack room the outline of the twenty-two beds, eleven on each side of the room were visible. I could not sleep and viewed what was to be my home for the next three months. One long room, beds each side sitting on white wood floorboards

"From where in the world does this white wood come from" I wondered?

We would all find out soon enough. Running down the centre of the floor was three-foot wide strip of mirrored lino running the full length of the barrack room.

"How did the manufacturers get it to shine so bright?" I would soon find out. Each bed space had a battle ship grey six- foot by three- foot steel locker. In the centre of the room were two large wooden racks with a large chain running through the centre.

"looks like a good place to store your water skis," I thought, that is if I had any. This was the rifle rack. At the top of the room stood three bright red buckets; two containing spotlessly clean sand, and the centre one containing crystal clear water. Under the centre bucket

A GUARDSMAN'S LOT

stood a highly polished brass pump and black hose.

"How did the manufacturers manage to get the brass so clean and the hose so black?" I was to find out soon enough. Looking around the room, the beds full of Britain's finest young men, most escaping Borstal or a father who enjoys the punch bag of a son and others like myself unable to get a job because I was too damn thick, and a lazy little bastard at school or so I was told. However, there we all were, twenty-two young men all with their own private thoughts that first night in the finest Regiment in the British Army or so the recruiting Sergeant told us.

"What would tomorrow bring?" I would soon find out.

Welcome to the Guards Depot Pirbright Surrey.

"WHAT HAD I DONE?"

At zero six thirty hours on the button, there was some guy shouting at the top of his voice to get out of bed, hands off cocks on with your socks. There was that damn bugle again, this time a different tune. Twenty two little faces all looking for Mum to bring the tea in bed. Instead all we got was to get to the washroom and loos outside. The one strange thing I do remember is, that smell in the barrack room first thing in the mornings. "One" that can only be described as bad breath, but stuck in your nostrils. What a pleasure to get into the fresh air and make my way to the washhouse. Where there were showers, sinks, loos and two baths. This had to service sixty to eighty guys, all not needing to shave but doing the manly thing, running a razor with no blade over our little cheeks. Ablutions taken care of we put on our clothes from the day before. There was a buzz in the barrack room as if a night in the barracks had made us all more confident.

"Where are you from, mate?" Says, one lad.

"What a load of shit this is", says another.

"I am not going to stay here", says the ginger guy.

A GUARDSMAN'S LOT

"Paddy", we will call him, had made his bed and was looking around as if he had committed murder. We later found out that in the night he had pissed the bed. Lovely. We all now had someone to take our fear out on; "piss the bed paddy" would not last long in the Irish Guards. At zero seven hundred hours we made our way to the cookhouse. What must we have looked like, longhaired civvies. The cookhouse was a big wooden building; in-fact all the buildings on the barracks were wood in 1966. The cookhouse, as all cookhouses do, smelt really good with that good old bacon cooking smell. Pity when you eat it the smell does nothing for the taste. Hard fried eggs, bone dry fried bread you get the idea. The one main thing that sticks in my mind was the watered down fresh milk, which of course made the corn flakes wet but tasteless, just like eating wet cardboard.

Reg was our barrack room trained soldier. He was from around the FerryBridge area near Doncaster, and was in the Coldstream Guards.

The only comment for Reg was that he was a fair bloke, with a good sense of humour, although a lot of it took a while to sink in. The Army has its own language. His claim to fame, and any one who knew him will remember his sayings;

"Cigarette me."

"Light me."

If a cigarette was not in his hand in less than five seconds we all ended up doing twenty press- ups. We soon learnt to keep a pool of cigs for Reg. Even if we were gagging for one, no one would dare take from the pool for fear of death. Trained soldier Reg had told us to be back by zero seven thirty, for there were things to do.

"Get into three ranks", says Reg.

"Fuck off. I had a wank last night" says Scouscer.

Reg glared at him.

I wondered who had had the shaking bed last night? Now I knew. The rabble that was now lined up in threes, turned to the right and marched to the Quartermaster's stores. It all

A GUARDSMAN'S LOT

went like a well oiled machine. One kit bag, one suit case and away we went on the clothing issue merry go round. I think it took me four and half minutes to go from end to end. In four and a half minutes, I had been issued all the uniforms, boots and shoes that would turn out to be my designer wardrobe for the next twenty-five years. The next port of call was to the barber's shop. There were the usual comments,

"A little off the top", I said.

"Trim the sideburns", says Jock.

It all fell on deaf ears. There were four Army barbers who got through our twenty two heads in as many minutes. Short back and sides with a shine on the top. This was to be a weekly adventure for all of us. We all took the piss out of each other laughing and joking, inside we were crying. Bearing in mind this was the Age of Aquarius- long hair and hippies. There we were looking like twenty-two hard boiled eggs with a tuff on top.

"I will never go fucking out looking like this", Jock said, Whom was a big red haired Scot from Edinburgh? He had learnt the Army language well, from his big brothers kicking people's heads in on the streets of Edinburgh. I was to find out years later, that Jock was killed on a night attack on Mount Tumbledown in the Falklands conflict. The Scots Guards lost some good men on that Island fighting one of the only units of regular army troops to be sent by Argentina. Strange people the jocks. Time taught me never go out on a drinking session with a jock; if there is no one in the pub to fight they end up beating the shit out of each other. Its the normal thing on a Saturday night. Get pissed, have a fight, throw up and piss off home. In the morning all are mates again and no blame is ever offered. From the barbers of Seville we made our way back to the barrack room.

"Well that was a good days work" some London guy said.

A GUARDSMAN'S LOT

We looked at the time, and it was only just after nine in the morning. Was the Army really this easy? I was soon to find out. Reg pointed to an over large bucket that shone like it was chrome plated, it had a nozzle on the lip for pouring.

"You." He said, to me,

"Me?" I said.

"Yes, you! You little prick." Reg says to me.

How did he know that?

"Go to the cookhouse and fill that tea bucket with tea," Reg said.

My first order, and there was no way I was going to mess it up. I grabbed the bucket and started to saunter to the cookhouse, I heard a bellowing voice behind me saying.

"If you're not back in five minutes, stand by!"

I took off like a rocket, didn't want to mess up my first order. In the cookhouse the rest of the planet must have all been given the same order. Dozens of new guys standing around waiting for the tea to appear by magic in their buckets.

"There it is, in the urns from breakfast." Someone said,

Me not wishing to fail on my first order ran over to the urn and filled my bucket. Running and half flying back to the barrack room, I was the first to get the tea and the first back, what a clever lad I was. The rest of the squad had got out their brand new metal mugs and were waiting in anticipation for their lovely cup of tea. Apart from going for it, my job was to fill their cups as they stood in line. I managed to get half a cup for myself from what was left, which was cold with no sugar and tasted like cat's piss. No one else said anything, I got it, so, it was up to me to complain, that was my thought. Twenty one sets of eyes were looking at me as though I had just murdered their baby sisters.

A GUARDSMAN'S LOT

"Trained Solider" I said, "This tea is not good, but I did get it in 5 minutes like you said," I croaked.

"Where did you get it"? He said.

"Where we got it from at breakfast time," was my answer.

I knew what I was talking about my first order and all.

"You stupid little prick", Reg says.

Twice in one day, how did he know?

"That tea was made at 6 o'clock this morning, you are supposed to wait for the mess room trained soldier to issue fresh tea, idiot." Reg snarls at me.

My buts fell on deaf ears. My first order and all. I later heard that it was common practice that one little boy would be set up; the mess room trained soldier had a strange sense of humour. My learning days were just starting, as punishment for the tea saga I had to polish the outside of the tea bucket with brasso- so that was how the manufacturers got it to look so good. It wasn't chrome at all, just years of polishing! The arrow on the bottom had a date stamp on it 1954. How many little pricks like myself had run polish over this bucket, for getting it wrong? The next few days were a blur of kit issues, sorting out the kit into our lockers, all squared and pressed and laid out as per the photo. Our civilian clothes were parcelled up and sent home, the only thing we could keep was our underwear, but we still had to wear the issued, drawers Dracula. Soon it was time to meet our training instructors. These battle-hardened men with all the knowledge in the world, all called, "Sergeant". Each squad had one of their very own, his task was to drill us, take us from A to B and instil the knowledge. The first two to three weeks were drill, PT, drill, PT and cleaning the barrack room and our kit. We all now know how the manufacturers did it, its us. We were the most uncoordinated bunch within the regiments of foot guards and so unfit. Reg's job was to ensure we knew how to prepare

A GUARDSMAN'S LOT

our kit and the teaching of our basic personnel administration. He would show us how to fold our kit so that it would fit into our lockers, as everything had to be folded to precisely nine inches, then it had to be pressed and laid neatly on the shelves. We had red and white T shirts for PT with blue shorts, that came down to our knees, which made us look like right pratts. All this went on one shelf, blue at the bottom, white then red and then white again. Looked lovely, or it better had. Many a time Reg would look at your locker and then tip the whole lot on the floor.

"Fucking rubbish" he would say.

"Do it again,"

And that was only the one shelf, the rest of the locker would house all your kit, all lockers had to be uniformed. After a week of folding and pressing and laying out our lockers, and a week of lockers and kit being thrown around the room, we started to get the idea. The boots that we were issued had to be spit and polished, now this is a whole new ball game Only the army can buy boots with pimpled leather, so that we have to get a soldering iron and burn the pimples off! So now your good old size nines shrink to a size seven, no problem, squeeze into the boots, lace them up, and go and stand in a bath of cold water for half an hour, allow to dry and they're still size seven.

"Trained Soldier" says Brad.

"My boots don't fit" Brad again.

"Tough shit! I told you not to burn them for too long!" Reg shouted.

This was called Boning your boots. Years ago the Guardsmen in the past used to take a rib bone and rub the pimples, till they were worn away. Another method was to light a candle and hold your spoon over the flame, when the spoon was hot enough then rub like hell and this would work, it was a slow process but at least you didn't have to keep running into the bath with your toes curled up like some poor Japanese geisha girl. After the burning came the really hard

A GUARDSMAN'S LOT

part, you had to layer polish on the boots and rub it on with your finger, all the recruits would be running around for weeks with their index fingers looking like they had had it shoved up there arseholes. After the polish had dried on the boots then it was down to the serious side of spit and polish. You could either do it or you couldn't. Boy was I lucky, I could do it, Reg was a good teacher of this art, he brought his boots out for us to look at. I remember thinking that they did look like black diamonds. At this point in time we only had to "bull" "spit and polish" our toe caps and heels, with the overall plan being that the whole boot would have to be done by our six week drill parade. This was a test for us- we would be inspected not only how smart we were but on our regimental history. This was our night time activity, sitting cross legged over our beds, cleaning our kit. Reg would teach us about our heritage, and the great battles of wars gone by. So our six week parade was drawing near, we were all in a flap, if you didn't pass this test then we were not allowed to walk out- let loose on the town. Now the rush was on to get the whole of the boots done, I remember one guy tried to take a short cut, he had melted the polish and poured it over his boots. They shone like a mirror after he had bulled them. Well that was until he put them on, and as soon as he started to march, there followed him a shower of flaking polish. The poor guy had to start all over again. Over that six weeks period we had been taught a great deal; our lives were governed by kit cleaning, uniform fittings and of course the obligatory room cleaning. Now this was a whole new dimension in our lives, the lino down the centre of the floor was not for walking on, it was designed for polishing. Each room had a "bumper", a long handle with a 25 pound weight on the end and under the weight were small bristles. The polish was laid by us being on our hands and knees and then we would take it in turns to swing the bumper up and down the lino until it was like a mirror,

A GUARDSMAN'S LOT

and then start all over again until lights out. When the lino had too much polish, we had to strip it down with paraffin- health and safety went out of the window, candles burning, soldering irons and paraffin slopping all over the floor, luckily no one was fried-Pure luck. By 0800hrs each morning the room had to be ready for inspection, lockers open, beds all lined up, bedding striped off the bed and made into a square block, the room spotless. We never saw who did the inspections but when we arrived back at 1000hrs, the fear was that your locker was tipped out or kit thrown all over the room, with Reg stood there with his note book and pen. Any guilty party was made to have it all ready for nine thirty that night, where the duty Sergeant would come and inspect it again, and then if it wasn't good enough, standby for a major bollocking, and show again. Life was interesting in this thing called the Army. A very strange but understandable part of our routine was at bed check between 2130hrs and 2200hrs, was the foot and hands inspection by the duty Sergeant. You have to remember that some of these lads were real grotty bastards, not that they meant to be, they just were, their parents didn't know any better. "So" we had to stand on our beds, our toes at the end of the foot of the bed The Sergeant would stop at each bed and look at your feet and then say "hands."

You had to shoot your hands out in line with his face. He would check the backs of the hands and then shout "over" to check the palms.

If he found any offending dirt his drill cane (a stick that the Sergeants carried with steel tips) would come flashing down on the offending part. A squeal of pain would echo around the room. Some of us found this to be quite amusing, but we kept ourselves clean.

As the day of our six week inspection arrived, there were five squads to be seen and inspected; we were the second on parade. The whole thing would take about thirty minutes. I really must admit that we were all flapping.

A GUARDSMAN'S LOT

We had to get out of this place and relax away from the Army for a few hours. Our inspection started, the officer was looking for the smallest fault. He would walk down the line of freshly shaven faces,

"Finger mark on Brass buckle" says the Officer.

"Laces not polished," again says the Officer.

"Tie not tied correctly," says the Officer.

"Trousers not to the correct height," says the Officer

The trousers had to break at the 2nd lace hole from the bottom of the boot,

"Belt not fitted correctly," says the Officer.

We were sunk and there was no way that we could ever pass this inspection with so many faults, and this was only the start. God help us.

The foot drill started, with a great big black cloud hanging over us. Our squad instructor gave us a pep talk, what the hell, we had nothing to loose, so we gave it shit on the marching and saluting, we had to shout at the top of our voices,

"ONE- TWO- THREE- ONE," with every drill movement. By the end of our thirty minutes we were hoarse.

We were marched off the square and would not get the results till just before lunch. The time was dragging and we were paranoid, blaming the lads who got caught out for the inspection and the ones who turned right instead of left, we were doomed! All the squads got on parade standing in our three ranks. The Officer walks on parade, we all stand to attention. The results are handed to him by the RSM, we all passed. Now we don't have to shout any more, the ONE-TWO- THREE- ONE, could be put on the back burner. After that Friday session we had to re-clean all our kit, clean the room, and on Saturday morning we were permitted to be let loose on the main parade square with all the rest of the Depot recruits and Junior Guardsman's Company- what a shambles' we

A GUARDSMAN'S LOT

were. The only thing on our minds was the fact that we were allowed out for the Saturday night till 2200hrs. Our salary was approximately four pounds and five shillings per week. They would give us one pound a week, for our fags and cleaning kit, that really would be it, paid on Thursdays skint by Saturday. If you were lucky your mum and dad might send some extra cash. I do have to mention that Reg was really proud of us; he even stopped bumming fags for a few days. Strange though, after 6 weeks the little boy fat is replaced with lean tissue and muscle is forming on your ever aching body. There is a time when you're all supermen but you cannot see it yourself, you're just one of the crowd. After the six weeks inspection we were permitted to walk out as I explained, and were we looking forward to it. That means let loose on the civilian population of Woking, Guilford or Aldershot, from 1400 to 2200 Saturday night. The talk in the barrack room was who was going to score first. Remember we didn't even know the local area. But before we could get out we had to run the gauntlet of the Sergeant of the Guard. We were all dressed in our uniforms and had to march around the depot lines at a quick rate of knots, and then march up to the Guard Room window, bang our feet together and scream out your number, rank and name plus the Company that you were with. The Sergeant of the Guard had to inspect you. If you are not 100% clean, smart and tidy, the bastard sent you back to get cleaned up before he would let you go out. It was my turn to book out. Lucky again, off I went, with some of the lads. The two mile walk to Brookwood station was a breeze, all dressed in our new uniforms how could we not fail. This was before Northern Irelands problems and we were not targets for the IRA. Then as you know, this all changed and with it a way of life. A group of us went to Aldershot. We had heard it was the place to be on a Saturday night, as all the lady soldiers were there also. In the NAAFI club, the bar was open and in

A GUARDSMAN'S LOT

we went. No one asked if we were under age. Wearing the Queens uniform you were a man and that was that.

We all tried to out drink each other, but with six weeks of training with no alcohol passing our lips, so the beer stakes, takes its toll. I remember through a drunken haze beer cans flying through the air. The Parachute Regiment trying their hand grenade skills on us, so of course we had to show them we were trained as well. The grenade training came to a halt as the red caps arrived. We all left the NAAFI Club arm in arm with our lifelong buddies, the Para's. Well that's how it felt in the beer of the night, no one wanting to be locked up for the night. Dennis told me later that he had left as there was no chance of scoring in the NAAFI club and had made his way to Woking, where he went to the Salvation Army Meeting, to drink tea and sing hymns. Later he confided to me that it was all a bag of bull but he did manage to score, with the daughter of the Major, where did we go wrong? All we got was a couple of beer cans over our heads and a major hangover, trying to walk from Brookwood station drunk as skunks- the longest two miles in the world. We had to be in by twenty two hundred hours. If we were late we would all be for the high jump. Banging our feet together in front of the guard room window, giving the Sergeant of the Guard your number, rank, name and Company so he could sign you in, all this and trying hard not to act pissed, I am sure he knew, but the hassle of locking up 300 lads was too much bother for him, thank you. We staggered off to our barrack rooms and slept the sleep of the dead drunk solider. The following morning we were all suffering with major hangovers. Sundays were always the same- full uniform for church parade, it didn't matter what you believed you had to attend, Some guys tried to get out of it by saying that they were Satanists, no problem for them, march down to the church, stand out-side for the service to finish, and then march back with

A GUARDSMAN'S LOT

rest of us. So no one got out of it. After church we had to strip the room out and spring clean it, at least after church we were not hounded by the Sergeants and Reg was also quite relaxed. We just got on with it, after six weeks we knew what had to be done and got on with it.

On the Monday I was called into see the Officer as he had decided that I and Dennis were to be promoted to Squad leaders, no extra pay and no extra perks, but we had to ensure that all the jobs that had to be done got done. Now some of the guys didn't appreciate being told what to do by us, so I had to make my mark. One of the Welsh Guards recruits was starting to question every thing I told him to do. It became a battle of wills. I had by this time had enough of this prick so it had to be sorted, I had no other system open to me. I was really only the same rank as him, but had a one inch strip of cloth on my right sleeve. I resolved the problem one night, when he went to the bathroom I followed him, as he turned round to face me, he got a fist in his mouth.

I told him that if he ever messed me about again there would be more. I also suggested that he now settle down and no more hard feelings. It worked, there after the Welsh Recruit would do all he was asked to do. The word got out and there after no one messed me around.

The next six weeks were still drill and PT, but we now had moved on to being taught all about the weapons we would have to carry: the 7.62 SLR rifle, and the 7.62 GPMG machine gun. We had to learn these weapons inside out, stripping the weapons down and then putting them back together again. Many a ripped up finger during those early days, it was fun, it was why we had joined.

We were to get ready for the ranges, as it was to be the first time we had fired a loaded rifle. I really was excited. The SLR was the standard issue weapon of the infantry. It was a 7.62 calibre bullet/round as we called it. We had learnt so

A GUARDSMAN'S LOT

much, safety was one of the biggest issues. We all lined up to collect our ammunition, loading them with twenty rounds per magazine.

It was our turn to get on the firing point, the range officer gives the command

"WITH A MAGAZINE OF TWENTY ROUNDS, LOAD" (that's putting the magazine on to the rifle nearly ready to fire).

"DOWN. TEST AND ADJUST."

We have to throw ourselves down to the floor and get into a firing position laying on our bellies, at all times keeping the barrel pointing down the range.

"READY" (that's putting the bullet into the rifle, now it's ready to fire).

"AT YOUR TARGET IN FRONT CARRY-ON" (now we get to fire at the target). I see that it's a drawing of Russian soldier carrying a gun. Release the safety catch and we start to shoot. BANG! My shoulder is pushed back about three inches- still you always remember the first time. The guy next to me finds that his rifle does not fire, as he turns round to tell one of the Sergeants he tends to forget about the barrel of the rifle, which is now pointing at my head. The Sergeant, quick as a flash, kicks the barrel round to point down range, then proceeds to give the guy the bollocking of his life. His punishment was to run up and down the range with his rifle held over his head. Looking at this potential murderer, the sweat falling off him, taught him and us a very valid lesson.

Ranges over, it's now time to clean the weapons and pick up all the empty cases. Once finished the Officer has to inspect the weapons for cleanliness. There after we all line up, empty our pouches and the Officer walks down the line. We have to shout at the top of our voices,

"I HAVE NO LIVE ROUNDS OR EMPTY CASES IN MY POSSESSION, SIR!"

Then we all march off the range feeling like real men.

At the end of our total twelve weeks we had been trained, shouted at, beasted, fucked around from morning to night. Now we had to get ready for our passing "off" parade, that is where our parents are invited down to watch us change from recruits to Junior Guardsmen. It was a big deal for us. A big drill parade with loads of marching and foot banging. My Grandma came down to see me which was nice. The parade over, all went well, now were all called "Junior Guardsman", and my squad leader was no longer valid. We were granted a long weekend leave! So off home to Mum and Dad's to enjoy a few days rest. Now we could have our civilian clothing back at the Depot.

We all had to be back at Pirbright by 1800hrs, this was our big move, from the recruit lines to our new accommodation. No more trained soldier to look after us, now we would have to answer to boy soldiers who had been made up to junior NCOs. The rooms were the same long wooden huts and 11 people each side, the little room at the end was occupied by a junior Sergeant. Whose task was to make sure we did as he told us. The permanent staff would only get involved in our day to day training. Drill, weapons training, PT and other such soldiering stuff. We were expected to start and think for ourselves. Part of our basic training was the introduction to living in the field, that means braving the elements for twenty four hours. Not many people have ever had to sleep out in the elements before. It was late September of 1966 and we were sent up to Dartmoor, the weather was very nice during the daylight hours but as the light faded the chill set in, our task was basic. We were issued a brown box the size of a small shoe box, and a little cooker which contained what looked like fire lighters. We were told that they were called "hexamine cookers and blocks." The staff demonstrated the use of these strange contraptions. Put the block inside the tin holder, light the block, "which is a mission on its own" fill one mess tin "small pans with high sides" with water and place your tins of food into the water. The theory is as the water boils

A GUARDSMAN'S LOT

so the tins heat up, warming the food. All very simple really and after the food is cooked you have hot water for a cup of tea or coffee. Well it looked easy to us when it was being done by an expert his food was ready in twenty minutes. I really have to admit the ration packs as they were called were very good, stewed beef, mixed vegetables, tinned fruit, chocolate and sweets, matches, toilet paper, not the soft type of paper, but the grease proof type of paper, it doesn't wipe it only spreads. There was also: "Hard tack" biscuits, with margarine and jam, in little tubes. Also milk, tea, coffee and sugar. Overall, there is enough food, to survive for a twenty four hour period. It was our turn to become the cooks of the year, so we all set about getting our little gourmet kitchens ready. It was all so easy, "he says"! There were tins exploding and food being blown all over the unsuspecting cooks, I opened my tin of baked beans and got a jet of hot juice right in my face, The little tin openers that came with the kit were as much use as a chocolate fire guard only because we didn't use them right.

Jock asked me to sample his tea; there was a layer of melted grease floating on the top.

"No thanks, mate. I am a coffee man" I said.

Overall this lesson was to teach us that if you fucked up your food, you are the one that has to eat it. After the fiasco, the instructor told us that it could also be eaten cold, were we green or what? It was now time to clean up our mess. The thing about the hexamine blocks was that the base of the mess tins would be burnt black, and the stuff that was on it was a bitch to get off. There was a little steam near-by, so we all trundled off to destroy nature, and washed all the crap off our mess tins. The greens would cry, all that toxic gunge going into the crystal clear waters of Dartmoor. We sat around talking crap and getting to know each other and then it was time to settle down for the night, just to see if we could hack it. Dartmoor being Dartmoor,

A GUARDSMAN'S LOT

the weather soon changed to a force 9 gale. By 0300hrs it was wind with icy rain. Well there we all were, huddled together like lost sheep. We took out our poncho's "water proof ground sheets" and covered ourselves the best we could. Talk about a group hug, the weakest got shoved to the outer edge and froze, the strong were still cold in the middle of the huddle. The most amusing aspect about our first night out in the bleak weather was: the stupid platoon commander. He was only in his shirt sleeves, thinking he would stay cool in the day. So our leader of the day, went off on his own, and we didn't see him till dawn. He must have frozen his tits off, not that we gave a damn. This blue shivering figure shaking with cold tried to hide the fact that he had been a total fool, by not being prepared for the weather change, but what did we know? All Officers were stupid in some way or another. At the end of our little night out, we headed back to Pirbright, a whole lot wiser and a whole lot more thankful to be back in our long wooden barrack room with nice heating if and when it worked. The first port of call was the cookhouse for a real meal.

As a junior Guardsman, we had to try and learn a trade- there were only a few to choose from. Drummer, and learn to play the bugle and the flute or drum, you could be a tailor, and learn to sew things, the weaker ones wanted to be clerks, and the handy men were to be pioneers. I volunteered to be a drummer. I fancied the idea of bashing a big drum, but there was only one problem, they gave me a B-flat flute, and I was not impressed. My bugle playing was nothing to shout about either. The bottom line was I was never going to make a drummer so long as I had a hole in my arse. I went and saw the boss of the Corps of Drums, and requested a change of training.

"Thank fuck" he said, "and I thought I was going to be stuck with you forever."

So now I was to be a tailor. The tailor's shop was a small close knit community. It was all

A GUARDSMAN'S LOT

very laid back, but we were kept busy, turning up trousers. Me making coffee for the staff, cutting peaks on the caps "that's what makes them sit on your nose" me making coffee for the staff, you get the idea? Another part of our boy training was education, not at all like school, we were taught real things, like what NATO was all about, and real maths, so we could work out our wages. Talking of which! Now that we are Junior Guardsmen we got a pay increase, too. One pound and ten Shillings. We were still skint by Saturday. Every army has it bully boys, ours was the Company boxing champion, "Colin". He was a real hard man, and could back it up as well. He had been at Pirbright for over 18 months so he was deemed to be an old soldier. He was also the Junior boxing ABA heavy weight champion.

"His trick" on a Saturday was to walk round the rooms demanding "odds" (spare change) off all the guys. If you work it out, 100 boys all give a few pence, Colin has a good night out while we sit picking our arses. I have never been bullied and I was not going to start now! Colin walks into the room, we are busy doing our thing, and I had made my mind up to take a beating rather than give my money away.

He arrives at my bed-space,"

"Give me your odds" he said.

"No Colin, I wont" I say.

I must admit I really didn't want to take him on, but if I gave in I would be one of his bitches for ever.

"Think you're a hard man do you?" He says.

"No Colin. I don't, but you are not taking my money." I said, getting ready to get punched in the face.

"OK" he says and walks on.

"You're a brave little fucker, I give you that." he says.

He moves on to the next man. And I kept my money, he didn't bother me again. I did here a rumour that he was thrown out of the Army and jailed for man slaughter. That was after he had left the Junior Guardsman's Company. The routine was really cosy. Every 12 weeks we would go on holiday (leave) and because the army had been saving over 75% of our wages we would get a bundle to go on leave with. It was on one of these leaves that I decided to take a few days of my holiday in our Capital "London". My plan was to stay a couple of days in London, and then travel home to my Mum and Dad for the rest of my leave. I took the train to Waterloo Station., The "Union Jack Club" is just around the corner from the station, this was like an up market doss house for serving soldiers. Always get a bed for the night for a few pounds. It's much better today, but then, it was quite bad, the walls were all tiled in green and white, my room looked like a public toilet. The sheets were clean, so no worries. I unpacked my kit and took a shower. Luckily I was alone in the 50 man shower area. I got changed and went to the bar. I was nearly seventeen years old, no one questioned my age. I had a couple of beers and saw that the slot machine was not in use, some guy had been on it since I walked in, so I went over to it, put in sixpence and dropped the jackpot of five pounds. I got some strange looks from the patron's of the bar, so I cut a hasty retreat. While my luck was in I went over the road to the bookmakers, I didn't have a clue what I was doing so I put a pound to win on a horse called "Purple Silk"· it won! I walked out of the book-makers with more money than I had ever seen in my life a whole thirty pounds. I went into the pub called the "Wellington", just near the Union Jack Club, and started to get pissed. I met up with a guy called Reg, who was in the navy, he was doing what I was, having a few days on the town. He was a nice guy and we decided to go up the West End for a real night out. "Soho" was calling, "Soho" was the centre for dirty bars and topless waitress's even in 1967. My eyes were wide open or so I thought. I looked the part in my stripped trousers and stripped shirt with my brand new suede boots

A GUARDSMAN'S LOT

with my short back and sides. Off we went, we took the underground, already half pissed even before I started. We arrived in Leicester Square, really impressed, considering I had never been there before. We moved from pub to pub and then ended up in some seedy club. Ten shillings to get in and a free drink, we paid our dues and went in. What a let down, no topless waitresses, in fact we were the only people in the club. Some skinny "tart" moved in,

"Buy me drink" she said,

"Fuck off" says Reg.

I thought he was quite rude, till he explains that "if we had said "yes" she would have ordered a glass of champagne at ten pounds a glass, thank you Reg. We didn't stay long there. By the time we had hit the next bar I was well pissed. A sleazy ferret faced guy wearing a suite two sizes to big for him, asked us if we.

"Want a good time?" the pimp says

"Only a fiver," also the pimp

"Well why not," says I.

"Fuck off" says Reg.

I was really disappointed, but being a virgin I had no idea why I was disappointed. Travelling back to the Union Jack Club, I was starting to feel the effects of all the drink, no sooner had I stepped on to the underground train, sat down and I was being as sick as a dog. Reg told every one that I had food poising. "Yea right" I puked all over my new brown suede boots, they were ruined. We made it back to the Union Jack Club, the night porter had to find my room for me, I had only seen it the once when I was sober, but now I was as drunk as a skunk. He helped me to my room, and I fell into bed and I was gone to the world.

When I woke up I felt like shit, I checked my wallet and found that I was penniless, some bastard had come into my room while I slept and nicked my money. Luckily my train ticket was still there. I got on the first train to Peterborough and went home to see my Mum and Dad. I told Dad the story and he laughed and told me

"Serves you right, son" my dad said laughing.

He was right of course. All through that leave I was thinking I should have gone for a "good time". I would rather give a prostitute the money than a fucking thief. On my return from leave all the guys were telling their stories of: this bird and that bird, ..I kept my mouth shut.

Our final three months at the Junior Guardsman's Company we were elevated to be called the Training Squad. We were the old soldiers now, and I was then the Junior Platoon Sergeant, really the most senior boy soldier at Pirbright. This part of our training was going to be toughest so far, we had so much to learn, and we needed to learn all the skills that a man soldier had to know. Our instructors became animals overnight, we were beasted from dawn to dusk and then some more. Life was a pain, but our skills were getting better and better. We had to do section attacks with live ammunition and then full platoon attacks with live ammunition. Our battle fitness test was 10 miles in two hours twenty minutes, with full kit weighing about sixty pounds and all the platoon weapons. We had to go on our battle camp. As the platoon sergeant, I still had to do all that the guys did, we packed our kit and moved on to battle camp at Thetford in Norfolk. This was to be our final exercise for now. All that we had been taught until now had to be put into practice. We had to practice our ambush drills. Our Sergeant took us out on patrol. We made our way to a thick part of the woods that was covered in bushes and undergrowth. We had to crawl on our hands and knees to get into a position to see the little track in front of us. The Sergeant expressed the need for silence at all times. We sneaked into position, fifteen guys all laying down, facing the track with our weapons at the ready. It was a hot sunny day and in the

A GUARDSMAN'S LOT

undergrowth the gnats were having a field day on our exposed skin. The Sergeant had told us:

"No one is to shoot until I shout, FIRE!"

"Yes Sergeant" we said.

We had to stay still, movement would tell the enemy where we were. It wasn't long until the normal sounds of humanity can be heard, I big loud fart rattles the silence.

"Shut the fuck up", whispers the Sergeant.

Silence is restored, a couple of the guys get the giggles, which in turn sets every one off, stifling and choking on our laughter. Silence is the rule. We finally compose ourselves, with the heat and the tranquilly and warm surroundings, it's not long till the sounds of snoring are heard. We were laid there for hours. It is really boring. I must have nodded off as well, I remember opening my eyes and seeing the last four men of the enemy patrol, who are right in the middle of the track, and right in the middle of the killing zone. No one has shouted "fire" the Sergeant is fast asleep, I scream out.

"FIRE" and start to empty my rifle full of blank ammo into the ambush area, gradually the rest of the guys are doing the same. We kill all the enemy, funny even the ones that had left the ambush area fell down to play dead, job done. We pack up and move out.

"Thanks" whispers the Sergeant in my ear" You saved me from dropping a bollock".

"No problem Sergeant." I say.

I had now got a good ally.

Chapter 2.
Going Walkabout.

No one wanted to be "back squadded" - sent back to repeat the whole term again. So we all worked like Trojans. One or two of the lads didn't make the grade and were sent back to complete another three months with the upcoming training squad. On our return to Pirbright we were nearly home and dry, we only had to do the Commandants March and shoot, and the passing out parade, which I was going to Command. It appeared that when we returned we had been given a new Sergeant, this man was a total bastard. We had been in the army over two years, no longer little boys. On this one day, we had been on battle PT in preparation for the March and Shoot, and we were shagged. It was near to tea time and we were starving. This new bastard was stood at the top of the stairs, hands on hips. We saw that all our kit had been thrown over the road, and he was as mad as hell screaming and shouting at us like a deranged lunatic. We were made to run down the road to a given point, about half a mile from the huts, then to run back. He was telling us that we were useless and lazy and that he would make our lives a living hell, I believed him! The one thing that got me really angry, we had a lad who was a bit overweight, and this Sergeant was telling him that if he was last again we would all have to run again. So we trying to help him by hanging back to allow porky to get ahead. Well the Sergeant saw through this and we all had to run again. This sick game went on for over thirty minutes. When we were not running we were getting verbal abuse, or being told to

A GUARDSMAN'S LOT

get down and then get up, up-down-up-down-up-down, running around like men possessed. When he was finished we were all done in and bloody angry. This fucking man was not sane and we had two weeks to do. A lot of terror could be inflicted in two weeks. One of the lads said to me,

"Did you see his pants? It looked like the cunt had a hard on!"

"No I didn't see it" I said.

I went to see the platoon Commander, to report the man for his actions, I was told to just get on with it. "Wrong answer" I went back to my room, I had the little room on the end of the Barrack room this time. One of the permanent staff came in to see me, he agreed that the man was a total nutcase, we had to do something. But, What could we do? Our lives had gone from good to real shite in thirty minutes. That night when all the staff had gone home, I was hearing rumours of mutiny. The lads were adamant, they had had enough. This had to be thought through properly. We had seen our commander and got no joy from him. The fellow staff said that the guy was nuts, so as part of the team I had to organise the action to be taken. The mass walk out of the Training Squad was featured in the national press. I will now tell you the truth and not what the papers said, as I was there. At lights out all the guys were ready for bed, the duty Sergeant came in to check we were all present and correct, after the lights were put out, the whole platoon, bar a few pussy boys, got up and dressed into their Combat kit and we all met in my barrack room. There were forty six of us that refused to put up with this type of nonsense. After I had checked that we were all present, I made sure that we had red and white torches. The great escape was to start. We snuck over the road into the trees waiting for traffic to go by. All our field craft skills we had been taught were used to our advantage. Once in the woods I led the guys to the tow path of the old canal, and headed towards the main road in

A GUARDSMAN'S LOT

single file. We made our way towards Guilford in Surrey. We walked for a few hours. When we needed to get on the roads I made the lads show a white torch at the head of the column and a red torch at the rear, I didn't want any one getting killed or run over by anyone. Just on the outskirts of Guildford, we came across a small woody area, which had plenty of cover, with bushes and a lot of reeds. So I settled on this area as our hiding area. It was about two in the morning; I made the lads build little shelters from the bushes and the reeds, and then we all got our heads down for some well deserved sleep. If any one had seen us walking down the road, they would have thought we were just the army on a night march. In the morning I sent two guys to buy some bread and bits, it was like feeding the 5000, all the lads must have been hungry but there was no complaining. After our snack I got the lads together to discuss our options. We decided to sit it out for 3 days and then hand ourselves over to the press, and tell them the truth. All best plans sometime fail. We had been there about 48 hours and I saw a policeman coming over the field towards us. The jig was up, he asked what were we doing there, I tried to bluff it, he saw through it, considering we were on all the front pages of every newspaper in England. He called on his radio and within two hours we were herded on to the Guards Depot buses, the same ones that met me at Brookwood station two years ago. The buses took us the back way to the Motor transport area well out of the way of the press. We were met by our Company Commander and the RSM. Questions were being thrown at us from all directions.

"Amazing. Now they want to fucking talk to us" I said out loud.

"Tell them fuck all" said Alan.

"Yeah! Fuck them" said the guys.

I had to shout to be heard.

"We will only talk to the Commandant." I shouted.

A GUARDSMAN'S LOT

We were all placed in open arrest. That means that we can still walk about but had to parade at all hours of the day to answer our names. The guard room would not take 46 of us, so we were loaded back onto the buses and transported back to our accommodation, via the back route. The powers that be, made sure we were not seen by the press. The following morning at 1000hrs we were sent for in groups of five, they started with me as I was the senior one there. I told the commandant the full story, the Sergeant was sat there as well; I had no problems telling the story in front of him, as I only told the truth. I did not mention the erection as I didn't see it. All the other guys were called in, which took over two days, and we all remained in open arrest. After we had all given our statements then decisions had to be made by the Commandant. We had all agreed that if we were charged with "absence without leave" we would all ask for a court Martial. I had also informed the Commandant of this decision. I don't now for sure what happened to the sick Sergeant or to the inept platoon Commander, I would assume that they were removed from the Depot and placed on to another post. No one was charged with any Military offence. The supposed ring leaders, myself plus five other guys were punished by being sent, from boys service to the mans service depot to join a squad in their twelfth week of training, which meant, instead of only four weeks training, we had to do another six weeks at the depot, and we would miss out on four weeks leave. The only good points to this was that we were streets ahead of the twelve week old recruits that we joined, and we were put on to man's pay.

So we, "the dirty six" arrived at our new home, the "Guards Depot, 14 Company" Grenadier Guards. The rooms were still wooden huts but this time they were much larger. The blocks were called "Spiders" as they had six large rooms coming off the centre square block, so from the air they resembled spiders. The

A GUARDSMAN'S LOT

centre block housed the toilets and showers, which had to service well over 100 men.

It was as if I had gone through a time warp. I was back to my recruit training days. I had been used to telling guys what to do and here I was being told how to do the most simplest of tasks. But at the Depot you just shut your mouth and get on with it. The saying that we were taught early on in our service was "See all, Hear all and say Fuck all". It stood me in good stead and still does today, "Yeah, Right". The Guards Depot had only eighteen weeks to train a man from civilian to Guardsman, so the training was really intense and you were expected to learn, or get back squadded. I really had no problems, due to my two years experience, the other lads would rely on me to help them on any points that they were not sure about. I didn't mind this task, most of the Depot guys were much older than me, I was just coming up to seventeen years old. I would help sort out their kit for inspections, my drill was up to par and my knowledge would help the slower members of the squad. Overall it wasn't as bad as we had expected. I had to repeat all that I had done in the Training Squad. When we were at our sixteenth week, the guys that had remained at the Junior Guardsman's Company, having had their passing out Parade and leave, then had to join us for the final two weeks at the Guards Depot. It was good to see familiar faces.

"Dennis" who I had left behind at the training Squad, and was now with us at the Depot, told me that there had been "hell on", due to the walk out. He said he thought we had all been shot at dawn, as we were moved so quickly from the Boy's Company. In the eyes of the boys we were deemed to be the heroes of the day. The junior guardsman's company had to change after our little protest. Never again would bullying Sergeants be permitted to act like god over their charges. The ones that did were soon found out and posted back, from whence they came. So, the protest had not been for nothing.

A GUARDSMAN'S LOT

The last two weeks at the depot were filled with preparations for the passing out parade, and the final hurdle was the "Commandants March and Shoot". This was regarded as one of the most physically demanding things we would need to complete at the Depot. Fail this and you were back squadded and you would have to do it all again. The morning of the March and Shoot arrived there was a buzz of fear and apprehension in the Barrack room. We had practiced this so many times and came within one minute of failing each time we did it, the clock stopped as the last man crossed the line. So being super fit and out front would not mean a damn thing, it had to be a team effort. I will explain what was required: we would be transported to Hangmoor Ranges, that's three and a half miles from the Assault Course at Pirbright. We would be dressed in full combat clothing and full Battle order webbing, steel helmets and platoon weapons. Once at Hangmoor we would lay out all our kit empty all our pouches, strip our weapons, ensuring that every thing was uniformly laid out on the floor. The kit had to be cleaned to the highest standard possible, even a speck of dust in your rifle barrel would cost you points, we had a spare guy from another squad to run round and pull all the weapons barrels through to ensure that they were spotless. The inspection was to be conducted by the Commandant himself.

After the inspection you had ten minutes to re-pack all your kit, assemble the weapons and then get ready for the march. It was important that your webbing was fitted correctly. Many a Soldier will tell you of raw open sores on your hips or lower back, due to the constant rubbing of the webbing on your body. Of course with webbing, if it is loose then it bangs up and down when you're running, which makes it feel twice the weight. The biggest bug bear was the old steel helmets. These were issued in 1948, they didn't fit and were always falling in front of your eyes or strangling you as it dropped to the

A GUARDSMAN'S LOT

rear of your head, thank goodness they are now different.

Once packed up and weapons ready, the Commandant would say GO, and off you went. Why they call it March I don't know? You have to run nearly all the way to achieve the time limit that is set. The route we have to take is all cross country, there are three big sandy hills called, the three sisters, and they are killers, steep and sloppy if its been raining. The course is three and a half miles long, through woods and of course the sandy path that sucks out your energy. There are tree trunks laid over the route, boulders and shingle, it is to say the least, a nightmare. The route has claimed many broken bones, pulled muscles, twisted ankles, or men that have just dropped from sheer exhaustion.

If you got through that then the Assault course was waiting to finish what the run didn't do, The Guards Depot Assault course is renowned through all military circles, it was rumoured the US Marine Corps refused to do it. In the nineteen sixties, there were thirty seven obstacles that had to be negotiated, ranging from 12 foot walls, 6 foot walls, 6 foot wide ditches, swinging planks of wood stretched over water, stepping stones, nets that had to be climbed that were twenty foot high, pipes to be crawled through, barbed wire that you went over or under, ramps, monkey bars where you have to swing arm over arm. The major obstacle was a thirty foot trench with 8 foot ramps at each end and a rope hanging in the middle, which you had to swing on to get over the chasm. The problem with the rope was that the first man there had to launch himself into outer space to catch the rope in mid air and swing back to the ramp to enable every one else to swing over, drop off the rope and back you went. Then some other poor dick would have to fly through the air and try to get the rope. This technically was by far the hardest obstacle and could eat up the minutes, which of course you didn't have many

A GUARDSMAN'S LOT

to eat up. The assault course completed and then there was the shooting to get right, you could fail the whole thing just on the shooting. If you couldn't hit the targets, then you were no use in battle, no matter how tired you were. You had to get your breathing right and stay calm. The targets would popup anywhere, if it came up in your area then you had to shoot it down. It was not easy. The shoot finished, and then you start to relax and have a cup of tea from the urn that sat on the range. The results were worked out and then you would either go back smiling or cry at the thought of having to do it all over again.

Chapter 3.
The March and Shoot.

We had checked cleaned and double checked our kit, we had our slow men tagged and we knew who were the strong guys and the weaker ones.

Getting on the trucks that would take us to Hangmoor we were all quiet, with our own thoughts. The instructor who came with us,

"It's all now down to you," he said. "I can only observe and not interfere at all. Good luck and give it fucking hell!".

We got there, some were wishing we hadn't and that the truck should have crashed, so they could get out of the March and Shoot. No such luck. We were there and had to perform, there was no way we ever wanted to do it again,

"Its all mind over matter" someone says.

"Yeah, they don't mind and we don't matter" says Phil, who later went on to G Squadron SAS.

We all start to lay out our kit and stand behind it like statues, awaiting for the arrival of the Commandant. Finally he arrived at 0930hrs. The sun is getting warmer and we know that we are in for a hot one. Did I take in enough water? I tell myself to take a drink before we set off. But now I had to worry about the inspection. The Commandant starts, five of the guys are told to strip down their magazines, the RSM is to inspect the rifles, he knows what to look for. They walk to each man checking for cleanness and serviceability of his equipment, some points are raised and written in the black book, we don't really now how many points we have lost.

"Get packed up boys" the instructor tells us.

After ten minutes I have my kit packed, have adjusted my webbing and had a good slug of water. The heat was starting to make us sweat, and we hadn't even run a yard yet. The command was given,

"GO" and off we went.

"By the right, double march" the physical training instructor says.

The first mile is eaten up in about eight minutes. I am sweating, so far so good. We were making sure that the weaker guys were watched very closely, its all going well till we get to the first of the three sisters. The sand is like dust pulling at our boots, and makes us have to work twice as hard. We ran up the first slope, but the look-forward was the long slog to the top. One of the boys, Joe, was finding it hard going, so I grabbed his webbing and dragged him up with me.

"Come on, it will be down hill soon" I said.

A GUARDSMAN'S LOT

At the top we can see the other two sisters in front of us, they look daunting. Down I go with Joe in tow, we just allow the weight of our bodies to run flat footed down the hill.

"Only two to go, Joe." I said.

After a short run we hit the second sister. She is the worst, she's big and long with shingle running down her back. Halfway up the bitch, there is a tree trunk that has to be climbed over. It was called her "tits". I made a point of gripping Joe's webbing harder- this is going to be tough enough just for me, let alone pulling Joe up with me! We were not looking good, the heat was sucking away at our energy, our faces were red with sweat pouring out of our bodies, and our combats were now black with sweat. There was no way that I could run all the way up this bitch. I got as far as I could. Joe was pleading with me to let him go. Now I am hot tired and angry.

"Give me your fucking rifle." I said.

He handed it over to me.

"Keep fucking going Joe, or I will kick your fucking head in" I screamed.

This shuts him up for a while and we struggled to the "tits". I look behind and the guys are spread out all over the route,

"For fuck's sake! Close up!" I was now screaming.

We climbed over the tree trunk (the tits) and continued upwards. The shingle was making us slip backwards. Holding two rifles, the barrels were hitting me on the head, and each time I slipped they would bang on my helmet. I didn't care, the only thought I had was to get up this fucking bitch. She has a false top, you reach what you think is her head and there is another 10 metres to go. I was swearing at the cow, calling her all the names under the sun. Gasping for breath, telling Joe to keep up, I was going mad! If you had seen me you would have thought so as well. Ever upwards, then all of a sudden your body weight is halved and you're falling down the other side, allowing one leg to follow

A GUARDSMAN'S LOT

the other. This time Joe was not being dragged by me, he went flying past me screaming that he couldn't stop.

"Good" I said to myself.

"Now keep going." Me again

The final sister was the nice one as she allowed herself to be mounted and was gentle on your body. Still, she made you work to conquer her. I collect Joe who had fallen, face down in the shingle, with his face and hands covered in blood. It looked worse due to the sweat pouring down his face.

"Come on Joe, nearly there." I screamed

I grabbed at his webbing and hauled him to his feet. We both started again to mount the sister. We powered our legs, which were hurting so badly you were beyond caring. Amazingly we made the top, gasping for air. This is the point that we have to wait for the guys to catch up. From here to the Assault Course was mainly all down hill. Time was not our friend, and some of the guys were in a worst state than

Joe, I handed Joe his rifle and went back down the hill, and started to kick, punch and drag the rest of the guys up the hill. There was no fucking way I was doing this again. Finally we were all formed up again and jogging as a squad. Sometimes it helps, the rhythm of the boots keeps you going, as does the threat of death if you drop out. The last quarter of a mile and the assault Course is in sight. The staff are all there as well as the Commandant, I would have believed the Virgin Mary was there if someone had told me, we must have looked like the retreat from "Mons" judging by the looks of concern on the faces of the staff waiting to see us. Joe was still bleeding, but give the man his due, he was still there doing it. Finally we arrived at the Assault Course. We had to get into all-round defence, laying on the ground, weapons in a fire position. We were all puffing and panting, the sweat running into your eyes, stinging. No one gives a fuck. Then you're off again, running your arse off to the 12 foot wall.

A GUARDSMAN'S LOT

This has to be tackled by two men acting as ladders. You literally climb up over them, pull yourself up and drop to the other side the last two on top then hang over the top and pull the ladders up and over grabbing what ever you can. We had practiced this for weeks. One of the guys that had been ear marked to pull up the "ladder" had just dropped off the wall and forgot about the guy on the other side waiting to be pulled up. "Phil" was one of the "ladders" over 6foot in height and as strong as a horse. He did no more than push up the other ladder, run at the wall and pull himself over the 12 foot wall. Try it sometime there are not many men could do that. The Queen Mary went very well we all got over it and the rope was always sent back to the waiting hands of the next man waiting to swing like Tarzan. The noise that is raised from twenty men screaming in pain, with nothing to keep them going other than sheer will power, is deafening. The final ramp was in front of me, there is a nine foot drop at the end. I ran straight over it and landed in a heap on the floor. I managed to wind myself, so now I could not breathe. My body needed air, my mouth was grasping for oxygen, but I was not going to quit now I told myself., gasping and puking at the same time. We had worked our bodies so much the only way it can fight back is to make you puke. Most of the guys were retching.

"Come on, we have to get to the range!"

I don't know who said it as I was too busy trying to get my breath back. The range was five metres from the last obstacle. We made our way to our allocated lanes. We can only shoot at targets that appear in our lane, and we have limited ammunition in which to kill all the targets. On the range the clock was still ticking,

"LOAD"

"DOWN TEST AND ADJUST"

"READY",

"IN YOUR OWN TIME CARRY ON".

A GUARDSMAN'S LOT

These were the orders that we heard through a veil of pain. BANG- BANG and so the shooting continued, we were scanning our lanes for any targets that appeared. Lane one was not having much success, his targets didn't fall when hit. His rifle fell silent. I was next to him in lane two. It was nearly all over. Lane one would be the one that would cost us the whole thing. I shouted at him to shoot at his targets,

"No ammo left" he said.

"Fuck fuck fuck" I said aloud.

Now what should we do?????? I shouted out at the rest of the guys,

"Who's got ammo left?"

I got some response and told them to throw their magazines down to me. These, I passed on to lane one.

"Now shoot the fucking targets down!" I screamed.

BANG BANG- he was actually hitting the targets now and they were dropping like flies. He had not been able to control his breathing, but now with time to recover slightly he was doing it as he had been taught to do. Finally the whistle blows, that's it. We unloaded our rifles and had them checked and filed off the range. Every part of my body was in pain. I sat on the side with the rest of the lads while the staff worked out the points, had we passed? The tea was there, but no one wanted it. The RSM tells us to get formed up in three ranks. It seemed like forever till the Commandant tells us that:

"What an outstanding performance!"

He congratulated us on our kit and our determination. Then our hearts sank, the matter of the ammunition being passed down the line had never happened before, so had the rules of the competition been breached? The Commandant said,

"After reviewing the rules and considering that it's a team competition, and in combat you would do the same thing if your comrades were to run out of ammunition, well done! You have passed and if you had gained thirty seconds on the March you would now hold the Depot record!"

Thank fuck for that. We marched back to the Barracks, as tired as we were we still marched like we had just been on a summer stroll in the park. Joe went to the medical Centre and had four stitches in his hand and a couple of butterfly stitches on his cheek. The rest of the day was rest and did we need it! With that over, the only thing to worry about was the passing out parade. We all felt like we could take on the world.

That night we slept the sleep of the dead; most guys were in bed well before lights out.

Chapter 4.
The Passing out Parade.

For the last week before our passing out parade, we were the RSM's property. The drill square was to be our battle ground, and the RSM wanted his pound of flesh from us. He would make sure that he got it, the passing out parade was designed in such a manner that all recruits leaving the Guards Depot had the skills to be able to carry out the "Trooping Of the Colour" or as we know it "The Queens Birthday Parade". The RSM's task, with all his instructors, was to find the holes in our foot drill and our weapons drill and beast us until we got

A GUARDSMAN'S LOT

it right. Our hands would bleed from the sheer power we used to grip and strike our weapons, the noise it made when done all together was like a bullet going off. Until our 16th week we had to march with our arms coming in line with our shoulders, the RSM now tells us that the arms can be lowered to breast pocket height.

"This is to make the parade look more professional." He tells us, to put a bit of style into our marching, one of the lads goes overboard and the parade is halted,

"WHAT DO YOU THINK YOU LOOK LIKE?" Bellows the RSM.

"Sir, I was putting on a bit of style, Sir."says the guy.

"WELL YOUR NOT!" Shouts the RSM.

"YOU'RE MINCING AROUND LIKE A SATURDAY NIGHT WHORE!" Still shouts the RSM.

"CUT IT OUT," he says.

The guys were now creased up laughing. We nicked name Brian "the whore". I believe it stuck with him for years. Finally with all the shouting and all the practice, we were turning into well oiled drilling machine, our confidence was growing with each practice. Even the RSM was getting off our backs. The final day before the Passing out parade we were rubbish, and the RSM cool as any thing says,

"OK lads off you go."

We were expecting to be bounced around the square and hammered into sticky melting blobs on the tarmac. When we got back to the barrack room, I asked the Sergeant,

"Why Did he do that?"

I was told that the RSM with all his knowledge knows that a bad rehearsal means a good parade., At that time in my life this philosophy didn't make any sense to me at all. The night before the parade we didn't need to be told to get our kit sorted out, our families were all coming down to watch their little "Jonnies" Passing out Parade so the order of the day was: to be the best you could be. The Parade Officer

A GUARDSMAN'S LOT

(the man that inspects us and takes the salute) was to be Major General Bowse-Lyons, a very senior long serving officer. Our uniforms were sent to the steam press for ironing, then you have to check them for stains and that all the creases are where they are supposed to be. Our shirts had to be ironed, they had loose collars and the collar studs were always going missing, our trained solider always had some spare ones. Our best boots were taken out and re-cleaned. We had two pairs of drill boots, one pair for day to day drill and the other pair for really important parades. There really was no difference as both pairs had to gleam like diamonds. As the passing out troops we had to wear white Buff Belts (pig skin), these had to be spotless. The whitening we used was not rubbed on the belt as this would cause ridges, so the method used was to dab it on with water to get a smooth but dull finish. When the brass buckles and brass slides were put on the belt they would mark the lovely crisp white coating, so once put together it was very carefully touched up with the whitening. We even polished the back of the brasses, no one was going to find fault with us. We all mucked in to help sort out the chaps that were not so good at kit cleaning. I don't think anyone went to bed that night, as the room also had to be spotless, so that Mummy and Daddy could see where and how "Johnnie" lived for 18 weeks. All parents and guardians would be invited to look around after the parade., Most of the lads also had their girlfriends coming down, and Jeff surprised us all, and said: his wife would also be there. We didn't even know that he was married. At 2200hrs the Squad Sergeant comes round. This time there is no bed check as we are still hard at it. He looks at our kit, and advises on this that or the other. Which, we are all trying to sort out immediately; we are tripping over each-other to get it right. We are a team, and it shows. All that time working together has put something into us, could it be

A GUARDSMAN'S LOT

that we are men now? Ready to kill or be killed for our Country?

When we think that there is no more to be done someone shouts for help, the polish on his boots has just fallen off, the poor guy has spent days polishing them. He is beside himself,

"I am fucked. I am fucked," he keeps saying.

The boots are given to me.

"Don't worry" I tell him.

I use my method of "spit and polish" and in an hour the boots are set ready for tomorrow.

"Thanks Steve," he says.

"That's a pint you owe me!" I said jokingly.

"You bet" was the response.

By 0200hrs it is all very peaceful in the room; the guys are talking in whispers so as not to wake the whole camp. We are the only ones passing out this time, and it is not fair to rub the noses in it of the guys who have it all to do very soon. The conversations are mainly in regards to: Remember the time Joe fell in the Queen

Mary? Or the time that Bill did the left turn instead of the right, what about that Bastard sergeant X who beasted us for being lazy on drill, these were going to be the memories that these fine young men would remember for ever.

0630 hrs, the bungle sounds, it wasn't necessary for us as we were up and about, dressed in our work clothes. We had to just finish off the rooms and hand in our bedding to the stores, get breakfast, our last breakfast as recruits. We all went to breakfast together. All the other recruits knew who we were and were looking in envy at us, some were telling us.

"Well done," from the other guys.

"Good luck," from the other guys.

We needed it, after our rehearsal the day before, "which" was totally rubbish. "Well" too late to dwell on that now. In two hours we would stand or fall. After breakfast, we went back to our Barracks. The Sergeant was there all ready. He told us that our postings were to be told to us at 0800hrs outside the Company Office. The

A GUARDSMAN'S LOT

Grenadiers had two battalions, the First and the Second. We were all marched down to the Company Office, the Company clerk walks out and starts to read names off the list,

"Andrews first." Said the clerk.

"Black first." Says the clerk.

"Edwards second." The clerk again.

"Farrow first." The clerk again.

And so it went on:

"Rudge first." From the clerk.

"Smith first." Says the clerk.

So, I was to be in the first Battalion. Out of the forty guys on parade that day, there were only seven who went to the First Battalion. The second Battalion were under strength, so they needed the most men. It meant nothing to me then, first or second, who cared so long as we left the Guards Depot. Were told to get back to our room and get ready for the parade, we didn't need telling twice. By 0930hrs we were all dressed and ready to go; the staff were fussing around us like mother hens. Checking ties and laces, the Trained solider had a duster in his hand and was rubbing our belt buckles, just in case there was an offending finger mark, if we failed it would reflect badly on the staff, and we didn't want to let our selves down nor any of the staff, they were all pretty decent guys.

We were on the road ready to march on to the Barrack Square (Gods Acre) when the Platoon Commander steps us off,

"BY THE RIGHT." Screams the platoon commander.

"QUICK MARCH". He pitches his voice.

And we're off. We halt, form up, get our dressing (all lined up) and order our arms (rifle) and stand at ease, to wait for the Inspecting Officer to arrive. The band starts to play and we remain stood for about fifteen minutes. The big black car pulls up, out steps this guy in his gleaming uniform covered in medals. He steps on to the dais (platform) and faces us. By this time we are stood to attention with our rifles at the shoulder.

A GUARDSMAN'S LOT

"GENERAL SALUTE" Shouts the platoon commander.

"PRESENT ARMS", the platoon commander now screams.

CRACK-CRACK-BANG, from then on it went like clock work. The inspection started, and the General was followed by every one of any importance up and down the three ranks of Guards Depot Recruits which were passing out today.

"Where are you from?" I was questioned by the General.

"Peterborough, SIR!" I say.

We were told to shout at all times when asked a question.

"Good-Good. well done," was his response.

He spoke to most of the guys on parade. The inspection over, we had to March past in Slow and Quick time, the band playing our Regimental march as we gave the eyes right in salute to the General. In "quick time" it's "the British Grenadier" and in "slow time" it's

STEVE RUDGE

"Scipio". I was taught that in Junior Recruits sitting on my bed, cleaning my kit, over two years ago.

After the March past in slow and quick time, we have to come into line, and advance in review order. That's counting sixteen paces and halting with no words of Command, this could so easily be fucked up. It only takes one man to miscount and the whole thing looks a complete shambles. We all got it right, and the final "General Salute" "Present Arms" and then to the speeches and prize giving. I don't remember what he told us, I wish I could. What I do remember was that I had been selected for a prize, for the best recruit in "Physical training".

"Recruit Rudge!" The RSM shouts out.

I had to hand my rifle over and march out in front of every one to collect my cup. Which was taken off me as soon as I had received it, I could hardly hold a rifle and march at the same time clutching the cup and base. The parade over,

A GUARDSMAN'S LOT

we marched off in slow time, giving a final eyes right to the tune of "Auld Lang- sine".

Once off the square, I was now Guardsman Rudge. We had to get back to our barrack rooms to meet our parents, girlfriends or family members. There was so much to do, hand in our rifles and any other stores that needed to be left at the Depot, pack up all our kit from our lockers and get it into our kit bags and suitcases. The Squad Sergeant said to me that I would have been awarded the "best recruit" of the squad, but due to my little "walk about", it could not be. "Never mind. Eh!" The guys going to the second Battalion were to get a weeks leave before reporting to their new posts. The First Battalion guys had to move to the Battalion straight away. Consequently my family didn't come down. It would have been a wasted trip as they would have only seen me for a couple of hours, and then I would be off again. It was something I would have to get used to in the future. We all said our farewells and that was that.

Chapter 5.
It's a Mans World.

We didn't have to wait long for a four ton truck to take us to the Battalion with all our kit.

Needless to say a lot of the original squad dropped out and went on to other things in Civvy Street. One young man blew his brains out, over some tart that was cheating on him. I was seventeen and a half years old, fit, strong and ever confident in my soldiering ability, but still with a lot to learn. I'd been posted to the Most Senior Regiment in the British Army: The First Battalion Grenadier Guards, and they were already training to go to the Persian Gulf. Training was to take place at the British Army Training camp at Sennybridge, in South Wales. Seven of us had to climb onto the Bedford truck heading to sunny Wales- the new boys on the block. We were en-route to our first real live battalion training, in preparation for a tour of duty in the Persian gulf. I arrived at the Battalion. The training camp was all wooden huts, older than the ones at Pirbright. I didn't have a clue were I had to go or who I needed to report to. People were moving around, so I stopped one guy and asked for some direction.

"New boy, eh?" He said.

"Yes and I don't have a clue were to go." I said.

"No problem. follow me," he said.

I grabbed my kit and the rest of the new guys did the same and we followed this guy. He took us to a small wooden building which had written on the front on a Blue-red-Blue painted board "Battalion Headquarters". He told us.

A GUARDSMAN'S LOT

"Hang on a mo."

He then disappeared inside, and moments later a Sergeant came out,

"From the Depot are you?" The sergeant said.

"YES SERGEANT!" We all screamed together.

"You can cut that crap out," he said, "There's no need to shout I'm not fucking deaf."

"Yes Sergeant," we said but this time in a lower tone.

"Right. Follow me" he said.

We followed on, struggling with our kit.

"You two, in that hut", said the Sergeant.

"You, in that hut." (that's me) He told me.

"And you two, over there in that hut" Said the sergeant.

As I was approaching the hut that I had to go to, a couple of the guys were heading for the same hut. They did more than that, and grabbed some of my kit and helped me to carry it inside the hut.

"Thank you" I said.

They dumped my kit on the floor and wondered off to the bottom of the hut. I was feeling very lonely. The guys that I had trained with were in other huts, but at least there were two of them together, for moral support. "Me" I was just standing there like a spare prick at a wedding.

"What's your name?" A Lance sergeant said to me,

"Rudge." I responded.

"Well Rudge, I am called Grotty, and I will be your section commander. Let me show you your bed space."

We moved to the bottom of the room and I see a spare bed with a straw filled mattress on it.

"That's yours mate" he said.

"Thank you. Sergeant" I said

"My name's Grotty" he said. "Call me "Grotty" unless we are on parade".

"Yes Sergeant." I said.

A GUARDSMAN'S LOT

Feeling like a right dick, Grotty wondered off. I started to sort my kit out, and I looked around to take my lead from the other guys in the room. They were all wearing their combat kit, so I changed into mine. Grotty came back and told me that the Company Sergeant Major wanted to see me. So I followed Grotty to what was the Company office. There was the same blue-red-blue board but this one said "Number Two Company".

"Come in young man." The CSM said.

This man wasn't screaming and shouting at me! "I must be in the wrong Army?" Were my thoughts as I flew into his office and banged my feet together and stood rigidly to attention. He said:

"The Company Commander is not here today, so he would see me instead. Welcome to number Two Company, you're in number six section. Sergeant Grotty is your section commander. Go to the stores and see the Pay Sergeant, then get your kit and rifle. Listen to Grotty and you will not go far wrong. Go on, off you go."

I turned to my right and left.

I asked Grotty where the stores were, and he showed me where to go. I went into the stores banging my feet together again,

"Fucking stop that!" Someone said.

"Sorry." I said.

I was issued: five blankets, two sheets and one pillow case, a full set of webbing, five rifle magazines, a set of mess tins, a rifle cleaning kit, steel helmet with net and chin strap, a sleeping bag and silk liner, and was told that in the morning my rifle number was 101, don't forget.

"No, Sir." I said.

"Me a Sir? Fuck off mate! My name's Tony and I am only the fucking Storeman!"

"Ok" I said.

Grotty takes me back to meet the rest of the section, and in no time at all I am part of the team. The transition was made easy thanks to

A GUARDSMAN'S LOT

the guys of six section. The four weeks spent training in Wales proved to be just what the battalion needed for desert warfare. It rained for the full four weeks that we were there. We learnt how to dig holes in the rain, sleep in the rain, eat in the rain, and shit in the rain! It was a battalion custom that the final exercise would not be complete if it did not rain. I remember "Jeff", jumping into his trench that was chest high in muddy water with a smile on his face, saying

"at least I don't need to get out for a piss! Who would notice? Apart from which, the 10 seconds of warm water down my leg was well worth it."

By this time I knew enough that the officer corps were the wonders of man, who would site a trench in a river bed when it's raining cats and dogs. They really still amaze me today.

My platoon Sergeant was a huge guy called Mick, with an endless sense of humour and the skills and knowledge of a highly professional soldier. A battalion rumour was that when he was doing his platoon sergeant's course he stood in the middle of a lake in mid winter in Wales, and that is a cold place in winter. The enemy wanted to catch him and his words to them were:

"If you want me, come and get me."

The enemy not being of such stuff as Mick replied

"Fuck off and freeze to death."

Who went on their way, forgetting the hard bastard in the lake.

We went out to the training area each day doing section attacks, platoon attacks and Company attacks. I had never seen so much live firing in my life. On one of the attacks there were plumes of smoke and load bangs just 300 yards in front.

I said to Grotty

"Someone had been busy with the special effects."

A GUARDSMAN'S LOT

"Don't be a cunt, Steve. That's our mortar platoon and what you see are live high explosive mortar rounds blowing up." Said Grotty.

Shit, this was training Battalion style. No one mentioned that the bombs were scattering the sheep that only minutes ago had been grazing. By the time we had advanced to that area I saw at least five bits of sheep, or is it sheeps? Whatever it was there were bits of them blown over a 100 yard area.

We were out one day, and it was really pissing it down. On our way back to the pick up point, the stream that we had crossed was now a raging torrent of water. We had to cross over it, which was hard enough in just our kit but our platoon radio operator, Steve, had his full kit and a bloody big radio on his back. Steve took four steps back and took a running jump to get over the river. No such luck. He sank like a fucking rock. When he came up for air he had managed to lose his SMG (a small machine gun) and there was hell to play. Now we had to wait while Steve took his kit off to try and locate his gun. It was like bobbing for apples. After about half an hour Mick said

"Fuck it. you will have to come back when the river's gone down, and you better find the fucking thing or you will be in deep shit."

He did go back and luckily he found it 100 yards down stream. Nothing more was said!

What was fascinating was the field kitchen that the Pay Sergeant (CQMS) had to set up to feed his troops. The cookers were called number one cookers "burners". These were better than flame throwers, the burners would sit under a steel frame, so that the pots could be placed on top so the heat would cook any thing that stood over it. We always had "all in stew" and rice pudding, we also had one of the battalion cooks attached to our Company. You had to keep in with the cook so that you could sneak a bit of hot water to wash and shave in, failing which you were fucked and reduced to cold water. Our cook was called Gordon.

"How's the stew boys?" He would ask.

"Great, Gordon."

"Its lovely, Gordon."

"Fantastic, Gordon."

Would be the "brown nosing" comments that some of the guys would make.

The fact that it tasted like burnt rat didn't matter so long as we got hot water to shave in. Gordon could fuck up a cheese sandwich, his fried eggs were crispy on the bottom and runny like snot on the top. When any one did complain he would get really sissy and say:

"Well, you try it. I cannot control the heat on this damn thing."

Referring to the number one burner, and then stomp off sulking. We learnt not to piss him off as it wasn't worth the tantrums, because it would mean the pay Sergeant(CQMS) would have to do the cooking, and he could fuck up a hard boiled egg or burn boiling water. Keep cooking Gordon? There was one good use for the burner which I observed. The CSM was pissed wet through, but then again, we all were, and while the burner is on full blast the CSM stands on the frame. It wasn't too long until the smell of burning rubber could be smelt 20 yards away. The CSM deep in conversation with the Pay Sergeant was blissfully unaware that his boots were catching on fire and that there was a great mountain of steam coming off his trousers. Within 3 minutes he was hopping up and down shouting to get his fucking boots off. There was no time, so he ran down the hill and jumped in the stream up to his knees, so that was a wasted exercise on how to dry one's self. The theory was good, but no one dared laugh at the CSM as he was one of the hardest men in the Battalion. But also a real gent and it didn't bode well to piss him off, he was always straight with the guys.

Wales training concluded with 1001 men all pissed wet through getting back to the training camp and trying to dry their kit prior to returning to the barracks in Caterham. To get

A GUARDSMAN'S LOT

the battalion back from Sennybridge we were pushed into as few vehicles as possible. I refer to this part of my life as "the convoy from Hell." I was shoved into one of the Mortar platoon Land Rovers. Thirty miles down the M4 Motorway, the driver said he has to shit, so the Rover pulls up on the hard shoulder. The driver removed his overall off his shoulders as he headed down the embankment. Then five minutes later he was back and we set off again. After only a few miles later there was the most foul smell of shit. The Sergeant in the front said,

"Who's farted?"

No one was going to admit to that, so the comments were coming thick and fast. References to Xmas trees to be used as a pull through, and what had died? After a while the stink was getting over-powering, and the light humour was turning into hate for the foul smelling dirty bastard who would not admit to his own smell. The Sergeant finally screamed at the driver to pull over. The Rover stopped and we were ordered out. As we were all lined up awaiting the interrogation, the driver casually slips out of his seat and walks past us to check his vehicle. That was when the guilty party was exposed. There was a large brown stain on the back of his overall. In his rush to shit, he had pulled his overalls down, squatted and shat inside the overall, wiped his arse, thrown the paper away, pulled up his overalls, turd and all, and totally oblivious to it all, and carried on. That poor guy never lived it down. After the clean up programme, the trip continued.

Nearly into London, the driver still trying to make friends, started laughing and telling us that some poor bastard's lost their wheel. We looked out to see this complete wheel rolling past us. We are all laughing like fuck, that is until our trailer dropped to the road in a shower of sparks. No one was injured, but the driver was never spoken to for the rest of the trip back to Caterham Barracks.

A GUARDSMAN'S LOT

The Barracks must be one of the oldest Barracks in England, at one time it used to be the Guards Depot. It had a huge wall surrounding it, and rumour had it that it used to be lunatic asylum in the time of Queen Victoria. Well it was now back to its former use, the lunatics were back, us! The barrack rooms were huge, one room could sleep thirty men. Things in the Battalion seemed to be more relaxed, and lockers were as you wanted them, so long as the kit was clean and tidy. The first week back from Sennybridge, all the new guys, all seven of us, were told to go to the home service store to get our home service clothing. This was new to us, and we had to ask where the store was? It turned out be a huge warehouse with rows upon rows of bright red tunics, blue trousers, blue/grey greatcoats, and the pride of all Guardsmen, the black Bear skins. We had to be fitted out, so the store's Sergeant took out his tape measure and proceeded to check our body sizes, we were measured from head to toe. The store guy then disappeared and came back with a hand full of uniforms including the Bear skin. He handed it to me and said, "sign here. It will all fit, so fuck off and try it on!"

He was right every thing he gave me fitted like a glove. I was looking at myself in the mirror, who was this dapper chap dressed to kill in red tunic and Bearskin??? Grotty came into the room and said,

"Best I show you what needs to be done and how we clean it all."

The tunic had to have all the white piping rubbed with chalk and then beaten with a flat piece of wood, to remove any sweat marks. The bear skin had to be groomed. It was soaked in water, shook dry and then combed to its shape with a DA at the back, and a fringe at the front. Attached to the bearskin was a curb chain. This, Grotty took off and explained that each link had to be cleaned with brasso and buffed up with a soft cloth. "Thanks Grotty," I said

A GUARDSMAN'S LOT

"Good. Now clean it and I will inspect you in full guard order at 1200hrs."

He was in fact doing me a favour, the next day we had to go see the Adjutant in full guard order for an inspection. The Adjutant would take no prisoners when it came to uniforms. He passed me as ready for duty. Two of the other guys had to show again, that means, getting all dressed up again and hanging around to be inspected by the adjutant the following day. I found myself written up on the Company detail board as follows:

Rudge S. Buckingham Palace Detachment of the Queen's Guard. Friday 23 June.

That was only three days away. I had no idea what to do, so I asked Grotty,

"no problems" he said, "drill is set for tomorrow and they will teach you all you need to know."

The next morning after 0800hrs roll call, the RSM shouts over the drill square for all the Queen's guards to form up ready for guard rehearsals. One of the older lads took me under his wing, and I find myself tucked in the rear rank of the Buckingham Palace Detachment of the Queen's guard. The Company Sergeant Major explains what to do, and we practiced it until we could do it with our eyes closed. Then we practiced it some more. These duties were taken very seriously by the Guards in late nineteen sixties. There was to be no room for error. Friday morning came and we had one last rehearsal, got our kit onto the lorry and we got on the coaches to take us to Wellington barracks in London. We arrived at 0945hrs in time to check your kit and get dressed into our home Service clothing, ready to meet our public. At 1015hrs we were told to get on parade and it all went like clockwork. I made no errors and there I was mounting my first Queen's Guard. Inside the grounds of Buckingham Palace, complete with Queen in residence, how do I know? Well the flag was flying, that means she's at home. 24 hours later, the procedure was reversed, and

A GUARDSMAN'S LOT

I am "off" duty, "Job done", and feeling really proud of myself. There I was, heading back to Caterham, on the same busses that we used the day before. We arrived back and took the rest of the weekend off.

At this point in the regiment's life there was a great deal of nicking taking place. If someone stole your trousers from the drying room then you'd better nick someone else's, otherwise you will be the poor sod who has to pay for them. I really believe that there were men in the battalion that went every where with no kit at all, and they would just nick what they needed for that day and move on till the next requirement, and not give a shit who has to pay so long as its not them. It was a very dangerous thing to do in those days of barrack room justice. If you got caught you could guarantee that you would reap the whirlwind. There was one incident that comes to mind being the age of the hippy our blue grey capes that we had for Queen's guard. A lot of capes were going missing from all over the battalion. Someone was flogging them to some creep in Carnaby street for a fiver a shot. The hippy flower power love crew must have thought it was great, there was a great demand for them. Well one night, I was laying in my bed in Caterham Barracks and I was awoken by a terrible scream,, was it a sighting of one of the past Guardsmen lost in the Battle of Waterloo? No way! As my eyes gained their night vision I saw revenge being met out to the thief of Baghdad. I started to ask what was going on and was told fuck off to sleep or do you want some? I slept like a log. The following morning there was a spare bed space and some gobshite Guardsman in the hospital, the nicking of stuff abated for quite a while.

The battalion routine in the late sixties was good, do your duty and fuck off out. We all worked hard but we also played hard. The Guardsmen then were no more or no less professional than the present day Guardsmen, I would like to think that we were not spoiled by politics. There was

A GUARDSMAN'S LOT

still a breed of ex-war time vets still serving as Guardsmen that is WWII, in 1967/68. Fred was one such character. I met Fred one night in the beer bar, he had a parrot on his shoulder this man was old school, the nicest guy ever, until pissed, when he became the old lag and hard bastard no one could enter the bar without his permission and when you got it you had to buy him a drink. So I got in, and paid my dues and settled down to enjoy my pint of NAAFI special. Fred is full of it that night, he was trying to tell a story but his parrot was squawking in his ear. Fred had had this bird for six years and loved it dearly, he did no more than rip the poor bird off his shoulder and wrings its neck,

"When I say shut up, I mean fucking shut up!" he said.

There was total silence in the bar, Fred looked at his audience and at the prostrate parrot, then he burst into tears. At this point the bar seems to melt into every possible exit. No one wanted to be around when Fred realised what he has done. Soon after this Fred did retire and I hope he is still telling stories to this day, a fine character of a man.

Chapter 6.
A Long Way from Home.

We were now notified that our overseas posting, ready to move date, was to be in four weeks time. The battalion was a hive of activity: packing boxes and shipping them out to some far off land. Well not that far, the Battalion had confirmation it was going to Sharjah in the Persian Gulf for nine months, wives and girl friends not included. Then we all had to try and get two weeks leave, before departing. Number Two Company had all but finished its preparations, our desert warfare had been kit issued and every one sent on leave. When I went on leave my parents had gone to Middlesbrough to visit my Grandparents. So I went up there, to visit as well. I lazed about a lot and went to the good old working men's clubs that litter the Middlesbrough area. I was out one night in the Pub called the Woolpack, which was near to the bus station in Middlesbrough centre. There I was, sitting in the bar, and there was a commotion, two women were shouting at each other, one all ready with a bleeding nose. They moved out side and the rest of the pub followed. Me being a nosey bastard, followed. As I got outside I saw one of the women just about to bury her high heel shoe into the other poor woman's head. Ouch that must be sore. It was all getting out of hand. Now the blokes were starting to have a rumble, time I left! I jumped on a bus heading towards Saltersgill. I moved upstairs and sat down. No sooner had the bus pulled away and a young woman sits next to me. The bus is empty, so why sit next to me?

"Hello. My name is Angela." She said.

"What's yours?" She asks,

"Steve," I said.

We get talking, she tells me all about herself. How she is very good at the trampoline and will be entering a competition very soon, at Billingham. That she does a bit of modelling, I really didn't believe that one, although she was quite fit. Angela asks me if I would like to go to the club, where her Dad works?

"Yeah, why not" I said.

We have to go to her house first, so that she can collect something for her Dad.

"Ok" I said.

We get off the bus and walk the few yards to her house. She lived with her parents, the house was empty, we both entered,

"Come in, sit down," she suggested.

One thing leads to another and we are on the floor swapping spit (kissing), it got quite heavy. I was still a virgin, and I left a virgin, but a little lighter. If you follow my drift. We went to the club and met her Mum and Dad, I told her I was going to Sharjah,

"Give me your address. I will write to you." She said.

"Ok."

And she did for a while. That was a brief encounter and I never saw her again, "too fast for me". My holiday over I went back to Caterham and was one of the first back off leave, in the car park were three coaches on the barrack square. I didn't pay much attention to them, I wandered into my room and was just watching television, in came the CQMS.

"Rudge, what are you doing?" He asked.

"Watching telly, Sir," which was my reply.

"Is your kit packed?"

"Yes Sir. It is."

"Fancy helping me out?"

"What Sir?"

"I need someone to come on the advance party; Johnson is sick and cannot make it.".

"OK, Sir What day do we leave?"

A GUARDSMAN'S LOT

"NOW!" he said.

I had to rush around and within half an hour I was sitting on the bus heading towards RAF Brize Norton.

The coaches dropped us off and we hung around for a few hours and then boarded the VC10 jet on route bound to Sharjah. This plane has seats that face backwards, its said that in the event of a crash its safer, dropping from 25000 feet the plane would hit the dirt like a fucking dart, well we will not dwell on that to much. At 0800 the following morning we landed. As the door of the aircraft opened the heat wave hit us. It was like when you open an oven door with your face too close to the door. Walking over the tarmac to the reception hall I saw a couple of the guys faint in the heat. The RAF must be used to seeing this happen, as they had one of those little trolley carts. Two RAF guys scooped up the fallen hero's and drove them away. What the fucking hell had I let myself in for? On this trip, to think, I had only nine months to go. Christ, I was melting. We stepped into the reception hall and the good old RAF with the air con blasting. Don't worry lads said one of the air crew we are not quite into summer yet. God help us. We had to wait for our kit to be unloaded. On gathering our stuff we were told to go into the customs shed.

"What? The Persian Gulf is the arsehole of the world and Sharjah is twenty miles up it", said one of the advance party guys.

"What the fuck would I smuggle into this shit hole," he said.

We need not have worried, the customs guys were just standing around, drinking Coke. We dragged our kit outside to waiting Bedford trucks, threw our kit on the trucks and jumped on with it. The trucks had to take us the short ride to our allotted barrack area. The Battalion of the Royal Fusiliers that we were going to relieve had rigged up a speaker system at the start of their Barrack area. They lined the route and were all waving with their brown and

A GUARDSMAN'S LOT

bronzed bodies from their nine months tour of duty. The speakers were blasting out the song of the day,

"I am the god of hell fire, fire, and your going to burn."

I still remember those days every time I hear that song. No shit Sherlock. Driving up the road most people we passed had knowing evil little smiles on their faces, or were they just glad to see us? All would be revealed. Here we are in the middle of the desert, lines and lines of silver tin huts all laid out in squares, with a sandy square in the centre of the huts. Inside the rooms which would sleep six people, were light and spacey. Running along the ceiling there was a large round silver tube, from which could be felt a small puff of cold air, and a couple of ceiling fans. This was meant to be our air conditioning, we were really feeling the heat. So we had to run around and get our bedding. This time we were issued 2 blankets, 2 sheets, 2 pillows and 2 pillow cases. That was it for now. The fusiliers were still there and our job as the advance party was to ensure a smooth hand over of all the kit that the fusiliers were to give us. So they still were in charge of all the stores. That was until the Grenadiers got hold of it. My job was to get the rooms ready for the platoon for when they arrived. As the Fusiliers left so our boys would arrive, it was a sausage factory. I would grab some cleaning kit, sweep the rooms out, mop the floor, get the bedding and lay it out on the beds, so it was all ready for the boys who could arrive at any time day or night. The CQMS would give me my jobs for the day and I would be left to get on with it, he even stopped checking my work.

"Well done Steve" he would say.

I could not believe it. I had not heard my first name mentioned by an NCO ever, and I felt quite honoured. I would still call him "Sir", I was not that brave. As more and more of the platoon arrived my job was made easier. The CQMS would tell me to get the lads and show them

A GUARDSMAN'S LOT

what to do. I made sure that six Section had the best rooms, not too far from the shithouse and showers but not too close as to get the smells. The ablutions were in a separate block with no air con or fans. Taking a shit was the equivalent sweat loss of running 10,000 meters. We were in and out of the showers. While I was busy cleaning the rooms, I would only wear my shorts and sandals. Every 15 minutes I would walk into the showers and not bothering undressing, would have a quick splash in the shower and then I would continue my work, refreshed for at least 2 minutes. Finally all the fusiliers had left, and the Battalion was now officially the resident Battalion of the Sharjah Garrison. On the camp we had a tank squadron, some SAS boys, engineers and a gaggle of odds and ends. We all had to eat in the main cookhouse which was a sweat shop. On the tables were dishes of salt tablets and anti malaria tablets

"Just help yourselves" we were told!

The main thing about the food was that is was really crap. The eggs tasted of baby shit, due to the preservatives that had been put in them to stop them from going bad. That would have been better than the shite we were given. Just near to our billets was a little row of shops. We called it the "wog shop" then, today it would not be politically correct to do so, but this is my story and that was what it was called. No offence intended. It was owned by Gulam Hassan who was a very wealthy businessman. He had shops in all the military bases in the Middle East, he was always busy, no wonder his eggs were good. Most of our meals were eaten at the shop,

"One egg banjo please" (egg sandwich) I would say.

His food was good. There was also an Indian fellow who would come around the blocks, selling tea or coffee and even his hot chocolate was good. This chap would time it so that from 0630hrs to 0700hrs we could lay in bed and wait for his call, then shout like hell and he would

A GUARDSMAN'S LOT

come into our rooms serve us our brew and move on the next room. I bet he made a fortune. The same thing would happen at 1000hrs when we were on our NAAFI break. This time he would have cheese rolls, which tasted lovely. The other side line was the laundry service. Gulam would have it back the same day, the army would take four days, and there would be so much starch that you had to thump your trousers open, you could stand your shirt on the ground while dealing with your trousers. We would mount guards just as if we were in Caterham Barracks. Of course the only really good bit of ground not covered in sand was the parade square, this Gods acre was good old Blighty tarmac. The world would freeze over if the battalion did not have a parade square. When the last lot of guys arrived they climbed off the trucks the sweat soaking their shirts, their crotches were wet from sweat. I recall one chap bent down to pick up his kit and his whole backside appeared by magic, that'll teach him to wear tight bellbottoms. It was policy that we had to fly in our civvies. Maybe if we had to land on non UK soil we could all pass off as tourists, and end up being shot as spies. I am sure it makes sense to someone deep within the MOD. Once settled in our Barracks we moved into the acclimatisation stage, which consisted of runs, PT and more runs. On average, just standing around, the human body needs fourteen pints of water a day, let alone doing physical exercise. The beer bellies obtained in the UK soon melted away. One reason also could be the fact that in all this heat the flies were abundant in number causing most people to have the world falling from their bottoms (the shits) on a weekly basis. The medical officer was sick to death of shit, mind you so were we. The medical sergeant Fred was the first line of defence for any poor sod wishing to go sick. If you got past Fred's interrogation and got to see the Medical officer be assured the next move would be a coffin or hospital for life, his favourite saying was,

A GUARDSMAN'S LOT

"You're bluffing your way. Right?"

It was rumoured that there was one young guardsman trying to see the MO for about fourteen days. Fred's consistent bluffing your way, soon put him off. The pain soon went after a short while the young guy's platoon sergeant fronted Fred and the man got to see the MO. Three days later the guy was sent back to England, his mother none too impressed about burying her nineteen year old dead son by gangrene poisoning. There after the MO was more approachable, but then the fun had gone out of the game, who could get passed Fred? Who gave a shit? One bright idea that our Company Commander had, was there was an old building on the desert horizon which looked to be only a few miles away, ya? Lets have an inter-platoon Challenge, super! We should see which platoon could be there and back in the shortest time. To the Company Commander, if you're reading this I hope your balls are soaking in a bath of acid, you arsehole. Over 30 men at a time heading for a speck of brick on the horizon. My Platoon were the third to attempt this twenty mile round trip through that lovely sand gripping your ankles and making one mile feel like ten, in heat that would make the devil sit up and take notice. What a bag of bollocks. Only two made it back, and they were in a fucking Land Rover! That challenge was soon knocked on the head. Thank you boss, the lads thought it was lovely, mind you; you made it back didn't you along with your fucking driver pip, pip, what! As you can understand heat stroke, blisters and a near death experience, what the Germans could not do in 1939 this arsehole nearly achieved in five hours. God bless the fools of the world. I will tell you, that after a six week period we were doing this as a matter of course, some of us used to run it just to relieve the boredom I suppose the boss was right, "but before his time".

Chapter 7.
The Lackey.

We settled into our routine; when not in the desert or the mountains tabbing around, we were in the Barracks, doing what soldiers do in barracks. A new Company Commander arrived and took over 4 Company (support Company). I had been transferred to the mortar platoon and a notice came up on the board for this guy who needed a driver and bat man. Me being a smart arse thought great, I can get my driving licence out of this, so I volunteered to be his lackey. I was then transferred to number four Company and got the driving lessons and was

Trevor's star pupil. How I was assessed on my driving test I will never know, considering the only tar road ran for only four hundred metres outside of the Barracks. Thereafter it was all compressed sand all the way to Dubai. Well, I passed my test and signed for his Land Rover. Strange that, it's the bosses vehicle but I have to sign for it, clean it, and maintain it, still it was better than walking. The Major had been part of the Royal Household and had arrived in the battalion, as the only officer whose shit didn't smell, or so he thought. What an arrogant SOB to say the least. Now I was on a new adventure, surrounded by super doper, kit cleaning, bed making and being a general dog's body, looking back I wonder if my licence was worth it? Still, it was better than walking. Which reminds me of an episode prior to going to 4 Company. My new platoon sergeant, who just happened to be the Battalion unarmed combat instructor Sgt Fred ex-Guards Para. Hard as a rock, in his Para days he had had a mishap and needed

A GUARDSMAN'S LOT

a steel plate in his head. So here we were in the middle of running up and down mountains (Jebels, they were called there). In the heat of the day, with the sun shining down hard, all of a sudden there was one hell of a commotion and Sgt (the head) Fred was throwing stones down the Jebel at the Company Commander. The poor guy was very upset for what ever reason, so the Company Commander orders our Platoon Commander to go get Sgt Fred off the Mountain. "Sir", he responded.

The only other guy around in ear shot, with any rank was Corporal Steve.

"Corporal Steve, go get Sgt Fred off the Mountain", said the Platoon Commander.

A look of horror fell on our section.

"With all due respect, Sir, Fuck off!" Said Steve.

Steve was standing there with his hand held in the salute so as not to offend the young pup. A great debate aroused as to how were we going to get the hardest man in the Battalion, who had just had boiled brains for lunch, off the Jebel.

"Fuck him, let him die. He charged me last week for fuck all," was one comment.

"Shoot him! Saves me getting my neck broke in thirty places," was another.

"Get the MO" was another stupid comment.

The MO was 5 hours drive away at the barracks sipping his pink gins. I did give one suggestion, and that fell on deaf ears, give him a block of ice from the Company Commanders cool box. Silly to think the boss would agree to that, his cold drinks would get warm just like ours then. We cant have that. However nature is not so cruel as Sgt Fred eventually fainted. The ever expanding metal plate was too much for his skull to cope with. In came a chopper and that was the last we saw of Sgt Fred. He was a good guy and thankfully when back in normal climates made a full recovery. Still to this day I can see this rock hard man tossing stones down the hill calling the Company Commander

A GUARDSMAN'S LOT

a fucking Bastard, and a Company of tough Grenadiers all too chicken to go get him. VC awaiting, not I.

Back at 4 company I was driving around in the LandRover with the hood removed and I fancied myself as one of the beach boys. Except the beach went for seventy miles in all directions. The Lido, as it was called, was our little beach where we could go and relax, have a swim or just laze around. One of the best jobs to get was the shark watch fatigue. This meant a full day on the beach picking your arse. There was even a bar to help with the boredom. I recall one day there was a shark sighting. The warning was sounded, whistle blasts. You were fucked if you were under the water as you could hardly hear the damn whistle any way. So the alarm was sounded, and instead of the water emptying, the rest of the guys were rushing into the sea with knives, forks and or any bit of weaponry that could be put to hand. Moments later the screaming banshee sounds and a five foot basking shark was being dragged onto the beach. The poor thing didn't stand a chance. There was a comment passed,

"All we need is ten tons of chips and we could all be at Blackpool."

Even in those days you had your eco warriors, bitching about the cruelty. Save the whale Smith, was dealt with as only these people knew how, and was ordered by the Corporal in charge of the beach to dispose of the corpse or he would be charged with littering the beach. Smith was last seen dragging the shark back where it came from. I swear there was a tear in his eye. We of course were hoping it's mate might seek revenge and eat Smith. Thereafter, Smith's comments were kept to himself. At the lido the platoon would take day trips, when worked permitted. It was always a great laugh, the footballs would come out, and the 1966 world cup was relived, on that beach in Sharjah. The beer was always nice and cold. It didn't take long to get a great tan, and no-one was even

A GUARDSMAN'S LOT

aware of skin cancer. Even the top brass allowed us to be in skin order in the Barracks (no shirts on). Some of the guys used to fish off the beach, but I never saw any one catch any thing. On our way back to the Camp we would ask the driver to stop at the local town (Sharjah). Then, it was a one camel shit hole with only a stinking souk (market) as its claim to fame. The souk however was full of gold smiths and copper beaters. We all had rings made for us which cost only a few bob (next to nothing). Watches were still great value Seiko's at a snip. I have still got my Seiko from all those years ago. It's not working but I have still got it. There was one stall that sold blocks of Cannabis resin, the hippies at home would have loved it! It was illegal to buy it, but some strange law said, he was allowed to sell it, didn't make sense to me. The silks were one of the main items that we would buy cheap as chips and really good quality. Next to the wog shop in camp was a Chinese tailor. He could make any thing. I had suits made for 10 pounds and they would be ready in one week. My pride and joy was a silk shirt, with black silk collar and the rest was white silk. Today I would burn it, but in the age of the hippy, I loved it.

Right next door to his shop was the barber. Now this man knew his job. We would come back from tabbing around the desert and visit the barber for a hair cut and a shave. It was sheer bliss. He still used the old cut throat razor, and always finished off with a hot towel and head massage. I don't know what he used on our hair? It was called (Ice) but it really cooled your head down, the only draw back was that the flies loved it. So, you were always getting dive bombed.

The flies in Sharjah were everywhere. They became a nightmare, and if we had to eat when out of the barracks, we would have to cover our heads with a cam net, tuck our mess tin under it, and spoon the food into our mouths as quick as we could before the flies ate the lot.

A GUARDSMAN'S LOT

The latrines when in the desert, were something out of ark. About 100 yards from the little base camp that we would set up, we would dig a pit and put two or three square wooden boxes over the hole. The boxes had round holes cut into the top, which would all be placed in a neat row, which we would surround with a bit of sacking, and there you have it, one communal shit house. Zero privacy, but what the hell we were all men together. We would have a water tank which we would use for washing. This was the favourite spot for the scorpions to hide, and caution was always the order of the day when getting water. We still had Gordon as our cook and one day he went to far and the Company Commander had to get him changed. What the silly sod had done was when making the all in stew in the desert, he thought it would be a good idea to put cheese in the pot with rest of the stew. Well as we all know cheese melts and goes stringy. I will leave the mess he made, to your imagination. Gordon was mystified as to why?

Why was it was such a big deal? The Company went to bed with no supper that night, the flies had a feast.

Christmas was around the corner, and the RAF bless them, had laid on a flight back to the UK for some of the lucky guys who needed to see their wives and families. Lucky my arse! The flight had been airborne for about one hour, and the VC10 seating theory was going to be put to the test, when a huge ice ball had broken the windscreen. The plane had to drop from twenty thousand feet to ten thousand feet in zero zip seconds, as the cabin pressure was fucked. But of course, the heroes retuned with stories of great valour.

"Were you frightened?" I asked.

"No, not me. But the cunt sitting next to me shat himself, and he was stinking all the way to Cyprus." He said. "I was not frightened at all."

"and so on", it made for a good story, and the guys left behind, felt better for not going on that flight.

A GUARDSMAN'S LOT

Steve was on that flight and told me he was shitting himself, the only thoughts going on in his head were, happy fucking Christmas, and screw the RAF. At the end of the day they got a free few days in Cyprus and went on to enjoy their Christmas at home. We poor suckers left behind had to drown our sorrows in the NAAFI beer bar.

A group of us were sat around the table with cans in hand, conversation had gone dry, some bright spark had the idea of a little test of manhood. The NAAFI bar was a long low room with ceiling fans dotted around the room. Directly over our table was one such fan, and the control switches set on the wall by the door with settings one to five. The idea was to stand on the table and stop the fan blades with your head. In the haze of drunken stupidity it sounded like a bloody good idea. At the time Tanky being the only sane one present volunteered to man the switch. Wish I had thought of that! The winner would be bought drinks all night, bargain! We all managed the fan on number one, the thud on the head made me realise this was stupid and not such a good idea, yet the rest continued. I was called a yellow shit but was permitted to be the judge. with extra credit for whoever stopped it with the most flare and style. Brummy was always one for a test of manhood and walked into the bar halfway through speeds two and three. He asked the fatal question,

"What's the prize?"

"Drinks all night," I said.

"I'm in, set it on four."

"Let's not fuck around in good drinking time". He said.

I think most of the guys were relieved as one or two were showing signs of concussion. Brummy stood on the table, Tanky hit the switch. The fan was now going round like a spitfire prop. Brummy lifted his head, whack... flies off the table, The Winner! The fan is now on the floor, and Brummy, instead of free drinks all night spent 3 days in the hospital with a case

A GUARDSMAN'S LOT

of real concussion! He now had a major scar to prove he had won. We couldn't really help much for pissing ourselves in hysterics when the medics carried him away and the duty officer wanted to know what happened. We all stared poker faced and declared Brummy to be mad as a hatter and suffering with desert fever. At least his reputation was intact. If not his head. When he was fit to leave the hospital he was placed on a charge for rendering himself unfit for duty, we never heard the last of it.

In between all this of course there was the serious side to our being there and the soldiering side went on unabated in spite of all the little mishaps. It was really a very hard tour of duty, but what is life without the Brummies of the world.

On many occasions the lads would get letters from their girlfriends, dumping them, me being one of them. Angela was writing me, then said she couldn't any more, these were called Dear John Letters. The army being the army, we would display our Dear Johns on the Company notice board for all to read. That way it sort of helped to ease the pain, when your mates were taking the piss, but it always went around. What girl in the late sixties is going to wait nine months for all that free spirited love.

One operation that comes to mind was when we were flown to Bahrain, as the locals were bitching about the Cause-way that links the airfield to the mainland and had threatened to close it. On route there we were discussing the many ways to slot the trouble makers It turned out to be a big nothing we sat in some shite Barracks for a week and then flew back to Sharjah, complaints were abounding, dressed for a party and no one turned up, we took our frustration out in the beer bar, no fans this time. Our Platoon Sergeant had got his hands on a blue movie, so as a treat to the boys he charged us one riyal each, to sit in the cell like room six foot by six foot, no windows, twenty to thirty sweaty guys, and all just taking the

A GUARDSMAN'S LOT

piss, watching this super 8mm crap movie, it broke the boredom, and broke our pockets the Platoon Sergeant didn't need to worry about his mess bills for a few weeks, was it worth it?. The time had come for our leaders to announce that the Battalion would be going home soon to the UK and just to prove we could still do it a final exercise was to be the climax of our nine months in the arsehole of the world, the battalion vehicles were lined up by 0400 the RSM was to lead the Convoy of thirty vehicles to the exercise area to move off at 0430 Hours. At four twenty five there was a small patter of rain drops marking the sand, well would you believe it, in nine fucking months of no rain the battalion lines up for its final exercise and it has to piss down

"No breaking from tradition then" I said to my co-driver.

We set off, by the time we had got only two miles it was tipping it down, visibility was zero, I was just following the lights of the vehicle in front and so was every one else, the route to the exercise area took us along the coastal road, the poor old Regimental Sergeant Major could not distinguish between the sand road and the beach, the water hid all from view, being a good Grenadier with a schedule to stick to there was to be no stopping on his shift, on we went with the rain pelting down in sheets, soon the convoys of smaller vehicles were starting to fill with water, not from the sky but the bloody big puddle we're driving through, the first rays of dawn had appeared and the lead vehicle had stopped,

"Must be time for breakfast" someone muttered,

"I don't think so", I said the whole dam convoy was half way to the Suez cannel. "No stopping on my shift" was to go around the Battalion but not within ear shot of the RSM. The exercise was delayed but soon got back on track, it was to be a forty eight hour exercise, we had to climb mountains some on the guys were lucky and the

A GUARDSMAN'S LOT

choppers put them on the tops of the mountains, we built defensive positions by piling stones up to form a wall of defence, we had to cook our compo rations, and save our water, each section had what water they carried and that was it for the whole time we were out. The anti tank platoon were live firing along with the mortar platoon, it was a very impressive site from the top of my mountain. I didn't do much driving on this exercise; it was good to get out with the guys. The final battalion attack ended at the coast and of course the enemy were defeated, we never lost. After the final assault, the RSM tells us to form up on the beach facing the sea with the whole Battalion in line of threes, the Commanding Officer giving the word of Command,

BATTALION,

BY THE CENTER

SLOW MARCH,

nine hundred Grenadiers in three ranks slowly sinking up their waist in the lovely cool sea, we were all still fully equipped. "It was absolute Heaven". The drive back started this time in full sun and back to normal, all the time I had been driving in the desert I had not had any punchers, on the route back from Abu Dubai to Sharjah I managed to get six, that will teach me to tempt the Gods by bragging, still to this day I make no comment when I see a car on the side of the road with a puncture.

Chapter 8.
Shylock.

When I got back to the barracks I had to repair all the tyres which I had needed to borrow to get me back, that was a real pain. It would soon be time for the Battalion to move back to England but before you can leave , all the stores and vehicles have be sorted out ready for the new guys to take on, just the same that we had, had done for us. In between all the cleaning and sorting, I was catching up on my sun tan in preparation to look like a male model, "Yea Right", there was a Company competition to see who could get the best tan, so all sorts of concoctions were being used, it was suggested, to get a really good tan which would make you go black was to try vinegar and oil, it worked! But I was starting to smell like a fish and chip shop on a Saturday night. we never found a winner as no one could give a dam, we were getting ready to go home. The final laugh I had was in the last week before leaving: there was one of the guys in the mortar platoon, who was a real tight bastard; he wouldn't spend a penny he must have been worth a fortune. We nicked named him "Shylock". All the other attachments had out door cinemas, they would charge a nominal fee to get in, and would sell cold drinks, however there was always a deposit on the bottle, it was only about the value of three pence. When the film was over, most of the guys couldn't be bothered to take their bottles back for the deposit, "shylock" was like a vacuum cleaner, sucking up all the empty bottles and taking them back for the deposit's. So on this last night before Shylock was going to

A GUARDSMAN'S LOT

leave Sharjah, he attended the Tank regiment Cinema, to do his final vacuuming of bottles. The Regiment taking over from us had sent their Advance party over, so there were new faces on the block. The film finished, shylock is doing his thing, he didn't find any bottles,

"What the fucking hells going on here?" he says, nearly in tears.

Stood by the cold drinks bar with a hand full of bottles, was this "clone" of Shylock right down to the same ginger hair.

"There mine" "there mine" screams Shylock,

and rushes over to the new vacuum bottle picker, "we" "by now" are interested in this display of territory defence, Shylock is beside himself, he's pleading to the guy

"How did you do it"? pleads shylock

"Easy" he says, I have heard of your reputation for being the bottle picker. So while you were busy still watching the last ten minuets of the film, I was sneaking round lifting the bottles! Explains the clone

Shylock was in deep shock, the only way he could console himself was to keep repeating to himself as we walked back to the rooms, "was"

I have a "reputation" murmurs Shylock

"Even strangers have heard of me"? Says Shylock.

I suspect he was gutted, "Shylock" "could peel and orange in his pocket". He didn't go to the cinema ever again while in Sharjah. The new battalion were now arriving in droves, and our boys were leaving on the return flights. It was now my turn to leave so all done and dusted I flew back to RAF Brize Norton bronzed and a whole lot wiser for my nine months in the desert, which was a long way from home.

I had managed to save a few Bob (money) and with my driving licence, I was now in a position to buy a cheap car. My Dad drove me to Peterborough car auctions I had sixty pounds to bid for a car, I ended up with a Austin A35

A GUARDSMAN'S LOT

van "green" so now I had "wheels" there was no stopping me. I enjoyed my two weeks on leave, and drove back to Caterham Barracks to arrive at about tea time.

Chapter 9.
Getting Serious.

Nineteen sixty eight saw a lot happening in the United Kingdom, the biggest drama being the Northern Ireland conflict. The British Army were totally un-prepared for the situation, still using tactics of the nineteen forties in regards to crowd control. The thoughts were that the Paddies were the same as the insurgents and that they would be causing up-risings the same as in Singapore. Needless to say it was back to the drawing board, and be quick about it.

Of course we were there, and were posted to "Magilligan's Point", an old wooden camp in

A GUARDSMAN'S LOT

the middle of nowhere, a truly miserable place. The good news was that we didn't stay there long and due to the riots in Londonderry we were sent there. This was a bit better at least, as there were pubs that we could attend. Our accommodation at that time was in the sailors rest, an old doss house, which was located on the water front. After drinking and chatting to the locals in the bar we would say goodnight and our closing comments would be,

"See you all later."

After kicking out time, the ritual barracking and abuse would be hurled against our patrols or guards. When we said "see you later", we always did. The odd stone would be thrown, but nothing serious and we could always see them in the pub the next night and take the piss.

All this came to a sudden stop. The top brass didn't think it was right, us cavorting with the enemy. I believe to this day that if they had just left it to the lads the whole 30 year episode would have ended in 1968, with one big drinking session and a bloody good bar room brawl and that would have been the end of it. Well, in Londonderry anyway.

It all really changed, but the sense of humour still prevailed. Our leaders had the knack of keeping us in London for the summer and shipping us off to Northern Ireland in the winter. Over the years Christmas became a long lost fond memory. In the summer at Caterham Barracks we would continue with our roll of Royal Guards, Trooping the Colour. On one day we were the Queens Guard, going on duty, after our little show in the forecourt of Buckingham Palace we were marching to Saint James Palace. The "escort to the Colour" was at the head of the Saint James Palace Detachment of the Queens Guard, guarding the Regimental Colour (flag) and we were all marching up the Mall towards Saint James's Palace. When this Gob-Shite of a hippy thinks it will be fun to dance in the path of the Colour and the silly boy tried to make the officer look like a fool, (which he really didn't need to try hard to do). So the escort comprising of two Lance Corporals, their sole purpose in life to defend the colour, as they had done since the 1656, Lance Corporal "Alan" does no more, than to take his SLR (self-loading rifle) with gleaming bayonet and sends our stupid hippy friend into the middle of next week, courtesy of his rifle butt. Then continued to march on, doing his duty. After the Guards dismounted the next day, the Regimental Sergeant Major sent for Alan. Oh Shit, now I'm in for it, possible prison for assault, fuck this for a game of soldiers. We of course tried to convince him that it was still a hanging offence to kill innocent civilians, even if they wanted to fuck around with the Queens Colour. Alan waited outside the RSM's Office awaiting his fate. The RSM shouted for him to:

"Get in!"

"Well, I hope you have got your kit packed?" Said the RSM.

Alan was shitting his pants, his whole world was falling around his ears,

"What for, Sir?" With a tremble of fear that the condemned have.

"You're on Orders." Barked the RSM.

Its called "memoranda" in the Grenadiers.

"The Commanding Officer wants to see you, and right now" Continued the RSM.

Alan was marched to the door of the Commanding Officer's office, the Company Commander was there and every one walking past Alan were looking strangely at him, that knowing look.

"INSIDE THE COMPANY SERGEANT MAJOR", the RSM shouted.

"MARCH IN", The Commanding officer said.

"SIR!" Responded the RSM.

"LANCE CORPORAL, SHUN!" The RSM.

"QUICK MARCH" Again from the RSM

"MARK TIME" the RSM again.

"LANCE CORPORAL, HALT." The RSM screamed.

"LEFT TURN."

A GUARDSMAN'S LOT

The Commanding officer was one of the right stuff, Ex- Guards Para, had a bad fall, but was still a gent. He tells Alan that, "the Queens Equerry" was on the Mall yesterday, and reported to Her Majesty that you had performed your duty with the utmost professionalism, and up-held the honour of the Regiment. It is Her Majesty's Pleasure that I grant you one weeks leave, a smile crept over the Boss's mouth.

"March out, Sargt Major" said the commanding officer.

"SIR." Shouted the RSM.

"LANCE CORPORAL". Said the RSM "LEFT TURN. QUICK MARCH!"

Alan flew through the door into the passage, the realisation still had not set in, so he asked the Company Sergeant Major,

"What, does it all mean?"

"The explanation was given."

"But, Sir" He asked? "I beat some clown up last year and got 28 days, it don't make sense"

"What does son?" The Company Sergeant Major said.

"Now if you're not off these barracks by seventeen hundred you can forget it" the CSM smiled.

Did we feel like a bunch of pricks when he told us the story? There was one good thing that came out of it, and that was, all the Lance Corporals in the Regiment were looking to clop a hippy on Royal Guard.

Johnny and I were good mates, we used to hang out a lot together. I had the transport and we would go out to see what the local night life could offer! The local dance hall was called the "Orchid Ballroom", it was an old converted cinema. Saturday nights was live group nights, it was as you would see in the old sixties movies, all the girls dancing and the blokes stood around the edges drinking their pints of beer. Until they were suitably pissed to dance, I was one such guy, it was here that we saw two girls dancing.

A GUARDSMAN'S LOT

"Fancy your chances"? Says Johnny,

"Yea why not", I say

The beer having given me Dutch courage. We both wonder over and I say.

"Could we have this dance"? "Please", I say

Mine was quite willing but I saw on the face of the other one, "fuck me"! "Not another" "fucking Squaddie". But she finally said yes to Johnny, I think just to get rid of him. I was having a good time, Susan was pleased to dance with me, and we were getting on fine, I asked her if I could buy her a drink? And she accepted, Johnny was getting no-where fast, but we stayed as a foursome for the rest of the night. It turned out that Susan was a Nanny to two children, there father being a big diamond dealer in London, and Susan lived in the same house as the dealer and his wife. I remember the group that was playing that night "Chicken Shack" I thought they were rubbish but Sue liked them. On the last dance which Johnny sat out, I asked Sue if I could give her a lift home. It's OK she says I have a car, I thought well that's that five quid on drinks and nothing to show for it!

"But" "you can come back for coffee if you like" She says,

"Quick as a flash, "I say" "OK" "that would be nice",

"I will follow you then" I say.

We all left the dance and go to the car park, there I am with my clapped out old van and Sue in a brand new Mini. "Johnny is stuck" I am his lift back, due to the fact that the girl he was with, got in her car and fucked off at a great rate of knots, leaving Johnny standing in a cloud of dust. He was a good mate, so he played "gooseberry" (hanging around) for the rest of the night, we left after coffee, but not before I had secured another date with Sue. We left Godalming at 0200hrs and drove back to Caterham, Johnny was well pissed off,

"Fucking bitch" he says, referring to the girl that left,

"She must be gay"? says Johnny.

A GUARDSMAN'S LOT

I didn't argue, Johnny didn't take rejection to well. We had to be up early the next morning, to practice for the Guard Mounting. I continued to see Sue, and we became an item.

The Battalion was going to move from Caterham to Chelsea Barracks, now we could be "Sloanies"; this was a better Barracks much newer than Caterham. Chelsea, which was a two Battalion Barracks, so we shared with a Battalion from The Coldstream Guards, we really didn't mix or interfere with each other and kept ourselves to ourselves. It was nice to go on early morning runs through Battersea Park. The barrack rooms were much better than any that I had stayed in prior to moving to Chelsea, they were two man rooms so you had a modicum of privacy, I was still being the lackey for the Major, and used to spend a lot of my time at Windsor at his house, talk about slave labour, I would have to sleep at the local Calvary Barracks and then go to his house and clean what ever kit was required, I ended up doing the bloody house work as well, I "susspose" that was what was to be expected at that time. At least I got an extra £1.00 a week for my domestic duties. So in between Windsor-Chelsea and Sue I was a busy guy. It was while I was at Chelsea that I asked Sue to marry me, the ceremony at Redhill registry Office was quick and to the point my chauffer was John, and my limo was a Mini van with me squeezed in the back. It all went well.

Chelsea Barracks routine was still the same crap, Royal Guards, and doing what men do in the Barracks. The NAAFI and beer bar was a shared area, so we could see how the other half lived (the Coldstream Guards) The duty Officer and Piquet Sergeant had to ensure that the NAAFI was secured after closing, they would walk round the building and ensure that all the guys had left and then lock it up. One night there was reason to have a good laugh, the duty officer, on looking around the NAAFI, saw shadows on the snooker room walls, he

A GUARDSMAN'S LOT

told the Piquet Sergeant to investigate. Well, there it was, Drummer X (Grenadier) was stuck up Drummer Y (Coldstream) over the snooker table, both were locked up in the guard room, in separate cells and discharged from the service, the standing joke for a while was, when ever we walked past a drummer, we would mention a game of snooker, and ask if he had potted the brown lately. The Corps of drums never lived it down. One pass-time, that was investigated by some of the guys, "to gain extra cash or free drinks" was to go to the Golden Lion Pub known as the GL, a known pub for the gay fraternity, they could not resist the challenge to try and hook a lovely Guardsman, they were generally mugged for free drinks and or mugged for real, not that I ever got involved in that. There were lots of stories at that time, some rich guy would pay a Guardsman twenty quid to be able to sit there and watch him while the Guardsman, screwed his wife, I was told she was really fit and the Guardsman enjoyed it more than the guy paying the twenty quid. The other one that comes to mind was the old boy who would be seen picking up a drummer in his Rolls, the drummer always carried a bag. When we pressurized him in to a confession it transpired that the old boy would pay him fifty quid so the old guy would just want to be able to wear the Drummers Bearskin cap, and strut around the room with fuck all else on except the Bearskin shouting orders, well that was his story and we could believe what we liked.

"What ever turns you on", "I say".

The Drummer was always good for a loan of a fiver. There was one character we called, Jimmy the Click, Jimmy could be seen around the Royal Guards, Saint James Palace, armed with his camera, asking all the Guards if he could take their pictures, it transpired that Jimmy was arrested one day for making lurid comments to the guard on number two post, saying stuff like:

A GUARDSMAN'S LOT

"I would love take your picture if you were naked".

Later the Policeman at Saint James Palace told me,

the silly fart didn't even have film in the camera,

"What some people will do".?

One day we were on guard at Saint James and we had a Royal visitor, Princess Anne came to see how the other half live while on Guard, the guard room is no more than a large room crammed with beds, its not a problem really, as the guys work for 2 hours and then clean their kit and are off for 4 hours, so the Princes walks around and the guys have to introduce them selves to her. After she had left "Johnny says" did you see the way she spoke to me? "She really fancied me"! We just fell about laughing; Johnny was one for a joke. Johnny was soon to leave the Army, he had had enough and developed a back problem, which he said he was putting on,

STEVE RUDGE

I believed him, after a couple of months Johnny was discharged.

John who was one of the guys from six section in Sharjah. We had become good friends and he had got married and was living in Streatham just off the main London road. Sue and I were lodging with them, these were the bad poor days, I remember all four of us sitting around the two bar gas fire freezing our tits off, the highlight of the week was: each couple would take it in turns to buy six iced fancies (cakes) and we would sit around with a cup of hot tea and enjoy our little treats. This one day it was johns turn to get the cakes. Sue and I had been out for the day, I was telling her that I was really looking forward to the treat. We arrived home and settled down for the night, listening to the radio (no television).

"Well John" I say:

"I will make the tea and you go get the cakes!" I say

John is looking sheepish,

A GUARDSMAN'S LOT

"What"? "I say"

"Steve" "I ate them", he tells me.

I didn't speak to him for hours. He did make it up to us, he got them the next week, but so did I, so it was a double treat. It really was the pits in the late nineteen sixties. We were paid real crap wages and not looked after at all. The Officer Corps lived high on the hog. On the backs, of their charges. With all the Royal Guards we were becoming sloppy in our real roll of being a mean lean killing machine.

To keep our soldiering skills going the Battalion went to Kenya for a six week training exercise, the main Battalions Headquarters being at Nanuki, there were three other bases dotted around parts of the bush, and the Companies would rotate around these different areas. At this time my boss was with number three Company and was to go to Gathuru, at the base of Mount Kenya, this was jungle country. Our base camp was tented and in the middle of nowhere, our task was firstly to set up the camp and then we would be set for the rest of our training. Toilets were dug, it has always bothered me, that the Officer Corps have separate toilets to us minions, I am told that they don't shit like we do, and when they leave Sandhurst they all under go an operation on their arseholes: so the shit pits had been dug, we tied some good strong branches over it so that we could have some modicum of comfort in our crapping time complete with back rest, we made the officers crapper for them also, heaven forbid that an officer should dig his own shithouse, unheard of. There were times when the boss pissed me off no end so on one occasion I took my revenge, he was in his tent, The other officers were out with their guys, playing Tarzan in the Jungle, I went over to the officers loo and slackened off the back rest pole, time would tell, and I was very patient, nature can not be stopped, I made myself busy awaiting the outcome, then it came the shout that went through the camp, then total silence, until:

A GUARDSMAN'S LOT

"RUDGE GET ME SOME WATER". Says the boss

I wonder to this day if he knew, well he does now, doesn't he? If ever you hear the saying that the upper classes shite never smells, believe me it does, and it sticks as well. Another mission we all had to do was climb Mount Kenya, tabbing through the bamboo forest and ever upwards, the Company Medic was a guy called Chippy, the Company set off at intervals, we were to all meet up at the base and tackle the summit the following morning, Mountain sickness is cruel, most of the Company were suffering with blinding headaches, Chippys aspirin didn't last long, and tempers were short, we all made it to the base, the boss called Chippy over and told him to give him some aspirin,

"All gone sir", was his response,

"Then damn well get me some", says the boss

"Sir","all I have is a medical bag and not a fucking conjurers bag", was Chippys Response.

STEVE RUDGE

Poor Chippy placed under arrest at the base of Mount Kenya, what a crock of shit, still life goes on. We all made it to the top the following morning, and that was when fate caught up with me, I was skidding down the Glazier, went to jump up and my left knee went pop, that was me stuffed for a while, I made it back down the mountain but Christ my knee was sore, that was my tabbing days over for the rest of training, I could still drive, so that was that. I told you earlier that my Boss had been with the royal Household and we were told that Princess Ann was to visit Kenya, Lord Richard one of our Platoon Commanders, he was invited to have dinner in Nairobi with the Royal Visitor, The arrogance of the boss, he thought that meant him also, well the dinner jackets were taken out of there packing and pressed, it was decided that the boss would drive himself to Nairobi, good, it saved me being fucked around. After a while we got a radio message, the vehicle had broken down and I was to take a replacement to

A GUARDSMAN'S LOT

him, I got there and transferred all the baggage onto the new Land Rover, hooking his dinner jacket on the outside rail intending to hang it inside when the rest of the stuff was in, well he was barking to get a move on, he jumped in the vehicle and drove off, four hours later I had the idea that I had forgot something, I had, the fucking dinner jacket was left on the side of the Land Rover, its only a five hour drive over sand packed roads, with the bright red dust, that only Africa has, I was going to be in deep shit, I had visions of some local, running around in the dinner jacket, and what would the boss do for dinner, fuck it, there was nothing I could do about it now. On his return, I was sent for and called all the stupid bastards under the sun, looking around the tent I saw his dinner jacket,

"But sir" I said

"Its there", me again

"Yes, no thanks to you", says the boss

STEVE RUDGE

I found it, still on the side when I got to Nairobi, what was white will never be the same again I had to have a little laugh to myself, his lovely white dinner jacket was the colour of a council workers overalls. Later I heard that his trip was a waste of time, as they would not let him in for dinner as he did not have an invitation, it was for Lord Richard. The base rats at Battalion Headquarters, at Nanuki, had the pleasure of being allowed out to the local bars, from what we heard the Medical Officer was kept busy with the penicillin, courtesy of the local whores, it couldn't have happened to a nicer group. We nicked- named them, REMFS, "rear echelon mother fuckers." The best we could do was sit in the middle of the bush and watch the wildlife go by, with a can of beer in hand. It was a good trip

and most of us enjoyed the hard work. One of the guys had spent the entire six weeks sunning him self when time permitted, he was as suntanned as burnt toast, thinking that he could get a job as the model for some model agency, with two days to go before we left to fly back to UK, his whole outer skin started to peel off, leaving pure virgin white skin, he went from bronzed god to white freak in 24 hours, needless to say we all took the piss out of him. It was soon back to England and the Barrack routine of Chelsea. Susan had, during my tour of Kenya been allocated a little flat at Morden, nothing to shout about but at least it was home, "when I was there". When I arrived back from Kenya, looking forward to seeing our new home, I got home and needed a bath, I ran the water and jumped in to the tub, being a hot bath man I noticed that I was getting covered in white bits, they were in my hair on my bollocks and even stuck to my arse, they were every-where. I jumped out and took a shower. On closer inspection it transpired that the old tenants had painted the fucking tub with normal household gloss paint. What a dick.! Sue and I settled down to our married life, scrimping and scraping, we didn't go out much we couldn't afford to. I had had the van stolen while Sue and I were at the pictures one night, I got it back but it was wrecked, so I swapped it for Johnny's Ford Anglia it was one of the old side valve engines, Johnny had painted it black and orange. So my first trip out in it and the fucking engine blows up, I had to borrow fifty pounds off my Dad to get it repaired. I ran the Ford for a while but it was pissing me off, so I sold it to one of the lads, and purchased myself a Triumph Vittesse, this bloody thing was worse than the ford, that soon got the chop and so I bought a little run about a fucking great big 1962 mark 2 Jaguar, I had to pay the insurance by the month, and the fuel bills were killing me. I was really stupid when it came to cars. I took the jag in for an MOT inspection and it failed, the back end was rusted to shit, so that was scrapped, I got £15.00 for it. No wonder we never had any money. I finally got hold off Johns car, that served me well. It was an old black Woolsey 4/44. I was quite the city gent running around in that, I bet I looked a right dick really, but at least it was reliable, when I wasn't putting tin or wood on the floor by the front seats to stop me seeing the road beneath. I had changed jobs by this time and was the Quartermasters Driver, my old boss having been posted to Hong Kong.

Chapter 10.
Deutschland Beckons.

Northern Ireland was to be an annual event, away for four months at a time. The Battalion was due to get posted to Hong Kong, or so we thought, no such luck for us, Germany bound, posted to Munster. So now I could buy a tax free car, the only thing I could afford was a little Hillman Imp, We packed up our stuff and sent it to Germany, at the same time we had the Battalion to pack up, I planned my route that Sue and I were to take, and we set off for Dover, to catch the ferry to Zebrugge, the crossing was fine , it was when I found myself on the wrong

A GUARDSMAN'S LOT

side of the road with a huge lorry heading strait for me, that I realized I had better drive on the right of the road.

I went round Antwerp at least four times until I found the right road; all in all we arrived at Buller Barracks in Munster Germany safe and sound, if not a little late, I was lucky being with Len I managed to get nice flat, not to far from the Barracks, But, here was a thing, the married guys under twenty one were not entitled to have an Army married quarter, good enough to die for your country but "fuck off" we cannot house you or your wife. So a lot of the guys that got married would have to try and get private accommodation near to the barracks, I have seen some shit holes in my life, but not the crap that these poor families were expected to live in, "remember" until Maggie got into power we were the second class citizens, on pathetic wages, unless you were an officer of course, and what did they care that Guardsman Baileys, baby was bitten by a rat at home. These are one of the things that leave a bad taste. So I will not dwell on it, other than to say, that the only guy who did care was Len, he was, what we call an ex-ranker, having started as a Guardsman and made it through the ranks. A fine chap, and I know he fought many a battle on behalf of these guys and their families, it was a pleasure to work for you, Len. Germany was a real pain in the arse; we were a mechanised Battalion and had to use the Armoured Personnel Carriers "APC" as our war machines. I recall one time that I thought it was a useful aid to warfare, that was around the time that Guardsman Nutty , had decided he had, had enough of Army life and wanted to go home, so he does no more than jumps in an APC in the middle of the night and sets off driving around the Barracks , twenty five tons of steel and track, with the Barrack Guard running after Nutty, he was not going to stop for any one, a couple of the cars in the Barracks ended up looking flatter than a well used whore, fences were ripped open poles

A GUARDSMAN'S LOT

smashed, Nutty was running around for a good half hour, had it not been for the perimeters wire fencing wrapping around the track and dislodging it, Nutty would have been half way to Calais. Poor lad got twenty-eight days in the nick.

He was more lucky than what he thought, we were told later that the police had been informed and that if Nutty had made it to the main civilian roads the police would have shot him, I believe that, as the German cops take no shit, and certainly not from a nation that in 1940 flattened their town. After I had tuned twenty one, Sue and I moved into Married Quarters, "Robert Koch Strasse" which was much better than the flat but still quite basic but we made it our home. One of the guys had a little business going for himself, he would go out with a van on the last Friday of each Month. The Germans at that time would only buy New stuff, and throw away any of there old stuff even if it was perfectly alright and this was collected on the morning of the last Saturday of the month, so he would go round find any good pieces of furniture and then flog them to the young married guys, we purchased off him a nice sofa. The big thing to do for entertainment was to have house parties generally on a Saturday night, invite all our friends round and play some records and get pissed, with snacks included, it didn't have to cost a fortune as most people would bring their own drinks with them. Except for the tight arses who never got a return invite, and strangely enough, we never would see them have a party at their place. What was quite novel to us was, the fact the prostitutes didn't hid the fact, there was a street called "Semen Strasse" where the girls used as their meeting ground, we would take a drive up and down, not for business but because we had never seen sex so openly for sale. A lot of the single guys used to go to the local clubs, and always, there were problems between the locals and the Brits, many a fight and police being called in, the worst were the

A GUARDSMAN'S LOT

Military Police, they would arrest you just for being pissed and a bit loud, they were not liked at all. Germany was one long bout of exercises and barrack duties, the APCs would were require to be constantly maintained. The driver's job was the dirtiest job in the Battalion apart from the Battalion "Pig man" the battalion had its own pig farm. The exercises would consist of running around in the APC getting out and killing some imaginary Russian out post, it got really boring. It was time for me to stop being a driver and start to do some real work, so I left Len and joined number three Company. It was there, that when we were on one exercise in Soltau. And the Exercise had to stop at weekends, due to the fact that we were not permitted to move (APCs) the battle wagons, so the whole Company would sit around the camp fires with a couple of beers singing and just generally doing nothing. However the calm of the night was shattered one night by some thumping on our vehicles, and a whispered voice saying:

STEVE RUDGE

"If you want a fuck go to Sergeant X's tent" the voice said.

I was too pissed to get out of my sleeping bag so I passed on that one. However the stories that went around the next day were quite frightening and I was glad I stayed in my sleeping bag . Apparently a couple of the Sergeants had gone down to the nearest town, and picked up some local tart, who was a bit kinky when it came to , fucking British soldiers, they had managed to convince her that until she had been fucked by the true blue British soldiers of number Two Company of the British Grenadiers, then she had never been fucked at all. She accepted the challenge and was loaded into the land rover and smuggled into Sergeant X's tent. Well, as I was informed, about 12 men all lined up in true Grenadier fashion, and seniority, and proceeded to uplift the good name of the Regiment, by all intense and purposes she loved it, there was one point of the parade that I find hard to believe, but Guardsman Tony insisted it was true, and that was: that Sergeant X went for seconds after the boys had finished, and that this time, the noises of "a bulldog eating porridge were to be heard." Being married and all it was time for me to stop fucking around and get on with my career, I volunteered for the next Corporals Course, which was quite hard, the first few weeks consisted of us being taught drill and in turn us teaching drill, the theory being that if you can command a drill squad of men, then you can command anyone. The teaching method for drill has not changed in 300 years, and all the phrases have to be given parrot fashion, for example:

(THE AIM OF THIS LESSON IS TO TEACH YOU THE ABOUT TURN ON THE MARCH) "THE REASON WHY THIS IS TAUGHT" "IS TO ALLOW AN INDIVIDUAL OR A BODY OF MEN" "TO TURN THROUGH NINTY DEGREES IN SMART AND SOILDER LIKE MANNER") and so it went on lesson after lesson, I was really good at it and enjoyed the course, we of course had the obligatory passing out parade, each student was given a lesson to prepare and you had to teach it in front of the RSM and Commanding officer, the results would be given at the end of the drill phase of the course. My turn to teach a lesson arrived, it was to be "the Salute to the right on the march" It was one of the hardest lessons to teach, so much could go wrong, so I had resigned myself to give it all I had, and at least fail with confidence I said to myself. I went out and did a blinder, lady luck was on my side I remembered every word of command and all the moves, even if I say so myself, I was "fucking great"

The course result were to be given at 1800hrs that night, in comes the RSM, and reads out the results out of twenty seven men I was second overall; it was my mate "Wally" who beat me at the post. The next day at 1100hrs twenty guys are lined up to see the Commanding officer, ordered to attend for promotion to Lance Corporal. Seven guys failed. "So" Lance Corporal Rudge

A GUARDSMAN'S LOT

was born. The next part of the course, we had to do the tactics phase, that's the military side to being a leader, you are expected to lead from the front and know your men's weaknesses, we had to learn about tactics and why decisions are made in battle, how to give orders for a military operation, which have to clear and précis. The tactics phase was at Sennalarger training area. On our first night there, three of the guys had gone out on the piss, its about 2330hrs and the rest of us are in bed, I am woken up by a squeal of brakes and a god all mighty bang.

Someone says.

"Some fucking drunk twat has crashed his car"

I went outside, and just around the corner of our camp I saw the mangled mess of a blue car wrapped around a big tree. I ran back into the room and grabbed some blankets and shouted at the rest of the guys to give me a hand, when I got to the car it was a right mess, we couldn't find the driver till we heard a moaning some ten feet into the woods, the rear passenger was trapped in his seat the front passenger walked away with nothing wrong with him, he had been thrown out at the point of impact, however, not so good news for the driver he was in a right mess, I covered him with some blankets and did what I could till the ambulance took the two guys away. The driver was in hospital for over a year, the rear passenger broke his leg in two places. These guys were the ones that had gone out from our camp for a night on the town." Some night out" "Eh" it put a damper on the course, but the rest of us got through it and left Sennalarger a whole lot wiser.

Chapter 11.
An Instructor is Born.

I had no intentions of staying in Germany, and requested to go to the Depot as an instructor, which was accepted if I passed the instructors course, I worked really hard, bearing in mind that my knee had been out of action for some time, I learnt to live with the pain, and passed the course, there was also a method in my plan, to go to the depot as an instructor I would be promoted to Lance Sergeant, and get more pay. I found I had a flare for instructing and found that I could get the best out of my students, and achieve some good results, I always used to bear in mind what my Dad said, "Never ask a guy to do something you're not prepared to do yourself," I have used this and still do today, even though my Dads not with us anymore.

While I was on the course at the Guards Depot, Sue had to stay in Germany, the course was similar to the corporals course except it was really hard and you really had to know your stuff, considering that you would be teaching the future soldiers of the Regiments. I passed the course and drove back to Germany to await my posting order, and to get promoted to Lance Sergeant. Finally my posting was confirmed, so Sue and I packed up and moved to Pirbright in Surrey. My tour of duty was for two years at the Guards Depot, I used to run a disco on the side, so when the Companies were having a unit party, I would be called upon to provide the music, for a price, of course. On one occasion I was busy doing my impression of Dave Lee Travis, and some pissed up arse hole from the Cavalry Squadron thought it would be good

A GUARDSMAN'S LOT

news to take the piss, normally this prick would get a slap and told to fuck off, but I was working, I did advise him to watch his step and leave, and no more would be done about it, no, not this clown he went on and on, until one of his mates moved in and they left. What pissed me off, was, that during his mouth and threats he had caused the table to move and my, Blue Stacks record, Skiing in the Snow was scratched. The following morning I hunted him down, I found him still in his bed, with a major hangover, the look of horror on his face when he realized who I was, well I bounced him over to the RSM's office, and from there to the guard room, he learnt a lesson in life, if you don't know who you're abusing, "keep your fucking big mouth shut." The record ended up missing some time later, when my then ex-wife was sorting out hers and my stuff, hope you enjoy it Susan.

The rest of my fellow instructors Wally, Dave, Chris, and the Platoon Sergeant Johnny, our Leader was Tim , not like the other officers,

STEVE RUDGE

he came from Southern Africa and got a Commission in the Regiment, a good guy, who knew the strengths of ones none-commissioned officers, he later left the Army and went to the Oman as the Adjutant of the Jebel Regiment, The last time I saw Tim, It was as his best man at the Wedding of the year in Otterburn. Many of the Officers used the Depot as a two-year rest, one such little Rupert had a teddy bear, I lie not to you, this teddy had a name and was always with this officer, when on exercise, one day the platoon had had enough of this silly little shit, and stole his teddy and burnt it at the stake, there was no consoling him. Poor little bastard I am sure he had a tear in his eye. The officers at the Depot had really nothing to do, other than to be the Figurehead for the platoon, and to wander around waiting for the next cocktail party, or dinner night. Pip, Pip, WHAT! Public School educations, I believe the words "Bugger me" were banned from the officer training manual, due to the fact that if

A GUARDSMAN'S LOT

one were to, Shout, "Bugger me," three quarters of the regimental Officers would adopt the leap frog position, without thinking. One night I was on Guard at the Depot Guard room, the phone rings and my Corporal answered the call,

"Hey" "Sergeant get a load of this": he says.

I listen in for a while and hear this really sexy female voice, offering all types of sex, the Corporal declares his undying love for this woman and arranges a date. A few weeks later we are back on duty together :

"How did the date go"? I asked.

"Fuck that" he says.

"I drove all the way to Guildford", "and knock on the door, not only was she a fat sow, but stuck in a fucking wheel chair", he says laughing.

"That's a shame" I said.

"No" "not really Sarge, I still gave her one". He says with tears of laughter in his eyes.

"You dirty Bastard" I joked.

I changed his name to Corporal sicko. Wherever possible I would try and inject humour into the training to save boredom creeping in, the drill square was one such place, on emphasizing a drill movement, with the arms, I would say things like, "rip the arm away as if you were tearing a Zulu off your Mother," or, "lift your leg twelve inches and drive it down eighteen." All nonsense but invariably, it would get the point over. When I would meet my recruits for the first time my opening statement was: My name is, Rudge, you spell that: B-A-S-T-A-R-D, and I am the worst one you need to worry about.

"Where are you from Sergeant"? They would ask.

"I was born on a pissed stained mattress half way up the A1". I would tell them.

My mother would have died of shame if she had heard such a thing. Our Platoon Sergeant at the Depot was Johnny, Not the one from the first Battalion, he had already left, this "Johnny" was from the Second Battalion. He had so many little ways to try and make a few bob, one such idea was: Johnny's Service Centre.

A GUARDSMAN'S LOT

Johnny would charge thirty pounds for a full service on any car, he confided in me one day that all he ever did was clean the engine and put fresh grease on the battery terminals, he never did get any return business. A few years later on when Johnny was back at the second Battalion, he was the Motor Transport Platoon Colour Sergeant, his car was out of action "he must have done his own service" so he needed a car for the night, well without further ado he takes the Battalion Commanders staff car, all would have been fine, but as he was returning to Chelsea Barracks, some clown crashed into him, Johnny was never very lucky, the shit hit the fan. Poor Johnny found himself back to the rank of Sergeant.

Prior to my tour of duty ending at the Depot, I was by this time super fit, and requested to attend the Platoon Sergeants Battle Course, which was held at Brecon in Wales. The course, at that time was regarded to be the most physically demanding in the British Army, other than SAS Selection course. Prior to going to Brecon the Guards depot would run a pre-Brecon Training Course, so I got myself put on that, it was held at Thetford and we were taught by the guys who had all ready done well at Brecon, it was physically demanding but well worth the effort, I was even running in my own time, in full battle order, every one said I was mad, guess I was. So after the pre course it was off to South Wales and Brecon, we were accommodated at Sterling lines camp, which used to be the home of the SAS before they moved to Hereford.

The course formed up on the Friday afternoon there were about sixty of us started, the Aim of the course was to ride us till we dropped then ride us some more, thank God I was fit, that Friday afternoon, we were all issued our weapons, and told to go and get three bags of sand, if they didn't weigh five pounds each, totalling fifteen pounds in sand then extra weight would be given to us. The rules also stated that when out of our Barrack rooms, we would run everywhere, the only exception to this was immediately after a meal, so there we are sixty Sergeants running around the Barrack area like mindless nutcases, to be seen walking, would give you a miscellaneous F, that meant if you got three of these F's you failed the course. The whole of the British Army sent candidates to this course, which ran all year round, my course, started in November, any one who knows Wales will tell you that the summers are rain and the winters are freezing. We were ordered to attend a briefing, there, we were told that we needed to prepare our kit for the first of many Exercises, after tea on that first Friday, we mounted the trucks and moved out into the training area, where we are dumped on a side of a windy freezing hill in pitch blackness, and told to dig in, that means digging a trench five foot deep eighteen inches in width and four foot in length. What they had failed to do was issue enough digging tools, the normal allocation is each man will have a pick or a shovel, I believe this was done on purpose to give the "fuck-you-around" syndrome, this we would get used to in the next eight weeks, so there I am digging this fucking big hole on a hill of chalk, with my mess tin " that's a small tin dish for boiling water and for eating out of. Now we had another use for it, digging holes on the Welsh hillsides. The training wing staff put certain other students in charge and disappeared, to their nice cosy tent out of sight of us low life, scrabbling in the dirt. The first few hours were fine, it kept you warm to dig, and when you stopped the sweat would freeze on your body, causing the shivers to set in, so common sense dictated that you keep active. After a while the lack of sleep tends to catch up with you, and bearing in mind that the majority of us had been travelling all that day, just to get to Brecon, and strait out playing Soldiers all night, some time in the middle of the night we were given the order to move out, so now the night march started, it

A GUARDSMAN'S LOT

was the darkest night I can ever remember, due to the rain/sleet there was no moon or stars, it was blacker than a gorillas arsehole. It would have been like a comic strip cartoon, sixty guys all hanging onto the guy in front like a blind school outing, sounds would break the silence, as screams of terror would sound into the night, as some poor bastard lost his grip on the guy in front and stepped off into oblivion, falling down some mountain side. I don't recall anyone being seriously hurt, as we were unaware if they ever joined the line of "three blind mice", I am sure one or two were injured, apart from which! I didn't give a shit "so long as it wasn't me". The first rays of dawn were starting to appear, we could start to make out shapes, finally the signal came down the line to stop, it was like a train yard shuffle, each guy bumping the one in front. We were then ordered to line up, and we attacked a bit of an old farm building.

Which was a complete shambles, every one was worn out, finally the words we had been waiting for.

STOP. UNLOAD.

"Great" its all over, that was not so bad. "Well" what did I know? They gave us time to make a brew of tea, but no time to drink it, then we were off again. Only ten miles to go to the transport, this had to be covered in two hours forty minutes, any one behind this time and it was another miscellaneous F. We had to run and walk this distance, with all of the full kit, I won't bore you, but I came in second. Now we could relax on the trucks. I don't remember when we drove off; I was already snoring like a pig. Freezing cold, pissed wet through and didn't give a fuck, I had got over the first forty-eight hours. Over the next eight weeks there was no real fun in what we were doing, a great deal of running and tabbing, we had to write a full exercise this had to be done in your own time, it had to be so detailed that some lucky student

A GUARDSMAN'S LOT

would get to practice his exercise live, it was a huge under taking, it took me three weekends of constant writing to finish my exercise. My exercise was not used for the course. But for now the course had to stop for two weeks over Christmas, so we were sent home with loads of things to think about, Christmas day and I was running five miles in full kit and carrying a lead pipe that must have weighed twenty pounds. I was not going to allow my fitness to suffer, this course was far to important to me. And I had no intentions of failing. I did spend some time with Sue and did try to relax, and we even went to the Mess, for the Christmas Ball which was a real good night out, I have to admit I did get pissed that night, but went running the next morning. After our Christmas break it was all hands to pump and back to the course. Part of the training was the famous river crossing, our syndicate had to cross the river Usk in Early January, at 0100 Hours, it was snowing, and a trifle bit cold, to say the least, we had pre-

prepared our floatation packs in the barracks, travelling in the back of the truck towards our final destination, to the river of hell. The Army rules are, that this river crossing had to be conducted in total silences, some madman's idea of a joke surly? Ever tried to enter sub-zero water temperatures without making a gasping noise? So the first two guys cross the river, to secure the other side, we see them slide into the water and disappear into the darkness, after a while the signal is passed down the line for us to start the main crossing, the night is again pitch black, we are already frozen from the drive, not surprisingly, as we were only dressed in our shirt sleeves, no problem, we were going to learn how to be living blocks of ice! I slide into the river. In my mind I am telling myself, no noise, no noise, some loud mouthed bastard is going:

OOH-AHH-OHH-AHH, Its me!

The training staff are whispering for silence, the cold hits your body like a freight train

A GUARDSMAN'S LOT

slamming into it. It's strange but I was the noisy bastard making the noise. I swear to this day that it was totally unavoidable, the body cries out when its being brutalized, I made it to the other side of the river, as I am getting out my whole body is burning, strange I thought, then thirty seconds later I get the most gripping pain in my lower bowels, I have to shit, not later! but now! my arse hole is twitching if I don't shit now I will drop it down my wet trousers and end up stinking for the rest of the exercise, no way I say to myself, this war can wait for two minutes while I take a dump. I drop my pack, I loosen my trousers, I am rushing to a spot, that I am sure is clear of my comrades, drop my pants and the shit shoots out of my frozen bowels as if shot from a cannon, the pain disappears instantly. I am aware of being spoken to, it turned out that one of the first guys who came over the river to cover us, is laying in the bushes not six inches from the spot of sheer relief, his words today still echo.

"You dirty fucking bastard". The hero said.

It takes a lot to embarrass me, but this was bad, the wettest shite in the world, it stank like hell, and I unloaded it next to my mates head, in true Green Jacket manner, he held his ground, my apologies were never accepted, and frankly I don't blame him. After the river crossing we moved on, still freezing cold, until our tabbing warmed us up, but more over I was at least ten pounds lighter and able to tab a lot quicker. Years later I spoke to a medical friend of mine and he explained that the cold had set off a bowel spasm, and there is nothing you can do other than let nature take its course. I still feel sorry for the member of the Royal Green Jackets Regiment who stood his ground under the hail of friendly fire. It was time for us to go to Warminster to train with tanks and artillery this would take up a week of our time, it was an interesting week, we had to ride on top of tanks, direct artillery fire and map read around the area, overall it was quite laid back

A GUARDSMAN'S LOT

in comparison to Brecon. The remainder of my time at Brecon was one physical challenge after another, topped with the constant buggeration syndrome, inflicted on us by the instructors, or "staff", as we had to call them. Somewhere along the line, I must have learnt something or at least impressed someone, as I finally passed, with a none to shabby report, so now I was trained to be a platoon sergeant in the British Army. "What would" I do with this newfound knowledge? I do recall, the drive back home to Pirbright after the final exercise I made it to the M4 motorway but I was falling asleep on route, I found a turn off and pulled up, the next thing I remember was a knocking on the window, by a policeman, advising me not to park there as there was a band of gypsies around, who might steal my tyres, it was a good job the policeman didn't look to close, as the tyres on my car were as bald as a snooker ball, and no self respecting Gypsy would dare waste his time nicking them. Looking at my watch I was amazed to find that

STEVE RUDGE

I had slept for nearly 14 hours, Sue must have been frantic with worry, as I told her I would be home in a couple of hours, well it wasn't the first time, and it certainly would not be the last. "God Bless her." By the time I was due to be posted back to the Battalion they had moved to the Barracks just up the road from the Guards Depot, which meant I didn't need to move house, and then I was posted back to my favourite Company, Number two Company. This time I was a section commander with five platoon, I had been gone a while from this Company and some of the guys still saw me as Guardsman Rudge and were trying it on, trying to get away with certain thing that I was telling them to do, so I had to stand my ground, the very next bit of lip I got I put the guy in the nick and charged him with insubordination, he was let out and placed on Memoranda, he was threatened with nick but got seven days restriction of privileges. Which was enough for the word to go round that this was a new breed, and not to feed it crap or it

A GUARDSMAN'S LOT

will bite you. From Pirbright the battalion would do London Guards and Windsor Castle guards. I was pushing to do as many courses as possible I was getting bored with battalion routine, the next course was the "Unit Instructors course: "Nuclear and Biological and chemical Warfare" which was very interesting, the weapons that could be used on poor old soldiers is very unnerving, they are really nasty, we are shown a true film about a goat that has been subjected to Nerve Agent, seeing the twitching goat dying in agony really opens your eyes. I had a laugh in the mess that night; I was saying to this RAF guy, that if the animal rights people got hold of that film, they would have a field day. The RAF guy said "they don't use animals any more" I didn't believe a word of it. Every day we would be in the gas chamber with our Noddy Kit on (NBC suits) the wearing of the respirator was a nightmare you lost 70% of your ability to function if the weather was hot, the dam thing used to fill-up with sweat, chemical warfare would be a fucking absolute horror. its amazing, at that time you were expected to eat and drink, these drills were being taught to us, Who in there right minds is going to take off the mask to stuff your face with food with nerve agent or killer gasses floating around, I am convinced that if any lunatic was to use this type of warfare, the opposition would loose, it also has the knack of a sudden wind change and you're the poor bastard on the end of it, instead of your enemy. We went through the effects of what nuclear war would do, let me tell you the crap clothing issued by the Army would not be of any use, radiation will penetrate up to 10 inches of steel, that's why its stored in lead boxes. What they don't tell you is, that if your in the area of nuclear fallout, you may as well go and blow your head off, use this powder rub it on yourself to de-contaminate your-self, what a load of bollocks, your going to die and in fucking agony, with your hair falling out your skin bleeding your being constantly sick. Rub and dab the powder on, its fuller's earth, for fuck sake, you can go to the local garden centre and de-contaminate your self. I think what I am trying to say is: that it was a really good course, But it was a load of bollocks but we all had a good laugh. The instructors really believed what they were teaching us, I passed the course, and so now. I could be let loose on the Battalion. When ever I tried to teach the boys NBC I had to be really serious, they would wonder why I would suddenly burst out laughing, when I mentioned (rub on this powder) and that was me grinning at best, or a full scale laugh. Luckily I didn't do many (NBC) lessons.

Chapter 12.
A Long Hot Summer.

In the summer of 1975. If you recall it was red hot, so due to the low manning levels we had to do 48-hour duties on Windsor castle. This was over a weekend, opposite the castle is a hotel and the guardroom window looks over the road towards the hotel. This one night Tanky shouts for us to

"Come see" says Tanky

so all the guys not on sentry followed Tanky up to the roof, along the old battlements, looking down over the road and we had the perfect vantage point, with 10 pair of eyes viewing the

A GUARDSMAN'S LOT

happenings of the hotel room opposite, with the windows and curtains wide open, offering us the fly on the wall vantage point to watch the sexual exploits of Mr and Mrs X. Mr X, had the prowess of a porn king and his back side was going like a fiddlers elbow, on completion of his duties, he was shocked to hear applause and cheers, and comments shouted over the road,

"Good one mate" the guard

"Well done old chap" I said

"Christ she must be sore" the guard

All these comments from the Windsor Castle, Queens guard, the curtains were soon pulled tight. If you're reading this, mate, you gave the boys, a little light relief on a hot summer night, thank you. That weekend on duty had it's moments, Her Majesty was in residence as well, and the guards at the rear of the castle would often see her walking the dogs. At the peak of the summer afternoons, the sentry's were in full sunlight and in ones tunic and bear skin it was really stifling hot. So, on this day, I received a phone call from the Royal Household, telling me that,

Her Majesty, thought! That Her Guardsmen were far to hot, and that we should consider moving them to a more shady area. says the voice on the phone.

"No problem, Sir", I said

The sentry's were moved, when Guardsman Smithy asked why he was being moved? I explained the case, his only comment was, "and so why don't you fucking move me to the fucking swimming pool" So I can cool off properly. His request was denied. But it was a dam fine idea. On our return to barracks on the Monday lunch time, our Company Sergeant Major had given us instructions that he would be doing a barracks inspection at 1600 Hrs, you could smell the anger,

"Oh bollocks" 48 hours on duty, in the stinking heat and now this silly shit wants us to fuck around with cleaning and polishing, Tanky was heard to say,

A GUARDSMAN'S LOT

"Fuck him", I said

So all the Company mess members that had been on Guard, went to the Sergeants mess for lunch. Well, you know what it is like, one pint goes into two and then three, and so it went on, at 1630hrs in storms the Company Sergeant Major, he must have had second thoughts as to his intentions, when confronted by 5 totally gutted individuals, one who was stood on the table giving his rendition of "Zulu Worrier" the Company Sergeant Major said: I will see you all at 0800 Hours Tomorrow, what did we care, we were all in the shit together, and well pissed. It should be noted that at 0800 Hours the next day, we were all looking for excuses as to why, and who to blame. As we knew we were in deep crap. The end result was a good Bollocking and a promise never to miss-behave again. Which we really, really meant. Well until the next time!

Chapter 13.
A Death and a Birth.

On top of our duties of Royal Guards that summer. We had to prepare for yet another tour in Northern Ireland. This time, when we were training it had to be taken seriously, as our old friends from the IRA had stepped up their campaign, and it was serious shit, we were going to the heart of Bandit country, South Armagh. I am not going to bore you with the technical details, but, we were there, doing our bit for Queen and Country, It was at a little piss arsed town called Keady, we were still living like tramps, within the location of the

A GUARDSMAN'S LOT

local police station, the IRA took great delight in trying to shoot or blow up the base. Our leader of the day was a young 2nd lieutenant, who meant well but couldn't command a piss up in a brewery. The call came through that there was a suspect car bomb. I was the senior person on the ground so it was my show to sort it out. The car was parked right in the middle of town; we set about cordoning off the area so as to minimise any fatalities. All was going well until the 2nd lieutenant arrived, running round like a headless chicken squeaking orders to the guys, who totally ignored him, it was left to me to calm him down, I took the young gentleman into a shop doorway, and explained the facts of life to him, at some point into the conversation, he wanted to look at the nice car, I managed to pull him back just in time, to prevent an engine block from removing his young arrogant head, needles to say he started to listen after that, I am sure he has developed into a first rate officer, if there is such thing!

Keady had its good points, on foot patrols we were always guaranteed a cup of tea from one of the local residents, who just happened to be a young good looking woman, tea was served and the patrols would take it in turns to ensure that the hearts and minds of the very generous lady were taken care of. Her husband never did find out why she liked the British soldiers so much!!!!!!!!!!!!!!!!!!!!!!!!! One of the guys was complaining bitterly one day that she must be part of the IRA as a secret weapon had been unleashed on him, it transpired that she had given him a really raging dose of crabs, and I wonder how many more? "And I don't mean the ones that you find on the beach" I do remember sick parade was well attended for a few days and that there was no mention to stop for tea, It was not well known, but a lot of information and counter intelligence can be obtained, from well placed observation posts, in the attic is a good place. Once in, your in, shitting in plastic bags, eating cold food, and trying not to get caught up with the antics of someone's bedroom. After a while the thought of a good sit down shit sounds good, wait till the house is empty then slide down to the bathroom and enjoy the full comforts of home, there must be many a family who were unaware that their toilets had been well appreciated. Benny was on patrol with his section of three guys, he sees a guy standing by there in the poring rain wearing a long coat, Benny approached the man , the man turns and sees Benny and the patrol coming towards him, he does no more than pull out an M16 machine gun and sends a burst of fire towards Patrol, they all hit the deck and return the fire, the terrorist runs into the court yard of the local pub, Benny is now on the radio to base, and we are running down the road to see if we can help, then two shots ring out, as we arrive to cordon off the area Benny is saying

"he's in there" "he's in there"

Indicating to the back door of the pub, which we were informed was closed for renovation.

STEVE RUDGE

I grab one of my men and do a Starsky and Hutch(smash the door and roll inside) through the locked door . I have to stop myself short, I was going to open up with my rifle, for a split second I saw movement in the room, in fact the room was full of late night drinkers, the bar wasn't closed at all, we had been given shit information, which could have cost me to kill innocent people. The locals were not being very friendly to us, I was being called a dirty murdering bastard, I had to secure the room and I told every one to get against the back wall with their hand where I could see them, the rest of my guys had turned up by this time, I told Chris, to keep an eye and watch my back, I had to check the toilets for the gunman, my heart was racing and pounding in my chest, bottom line I was crapping myself. The ladies toilet was first that was empty, I kicked the door to the gent's toilet it wouldn't open, and something was holding the door to prevent me from pushing it open, I gave a really hard shove the adrenalin was up, the door slowly opens, I see a foot and then a leg, and as I push further I see the body, the man is laying on the floor, with the top of his head blown off, blood and brains are spread up the walls, it's a right fucking mess, one of the pub patrons tells me to get a doctor, I am down with the man and trying to dress the wound with my field dressing, I thought he was still breathing, as I was giving first aid he died, I am still being told to

"Get a doctor", "you murdering bastard" says the local.

"It's not a doctor you need it's a priest". Says I.

Benny was lucky that night if he had walked his patrol round the other route, the gunman would have had a good line of fire and Benny and his boys wouldn't have seen anything. The drinking pub crew were also lucky that night; they nearly had theirs as well. The two shots we heard when we were running down the road to help, were from one of Benny's boys, he had seen a face appear at the window after the gunman had ran in the yard, thinking that it was him, the guy got shot for being nosey. The Company Commander and the CSM were in the area, and at the same time that our medic arrived who had been at the base watching television who had heard there was someone shot, he grabbed his medical bag and ran to the area which was only 100 yards in his shirt trousers and boots with also his rifle, so now the CSM sees the medic and stops him to ask him why he's not properly dressed and why he was not wearing his beret, by this time a crowd was forming around the pub, the medic is trying to explain that he heard that someone had been shot and got here strait away, the CSM put him in open arrest for his actions, to this day I don't understand some peoples logic. There was hell on after the event, ballistic tests on the rifles, court cases and so it went on and on Benny and his boys would be backwards and forwards from England to Northern Ireland for

A GUARDSMAN'S LOT

years to come. That was really only the main drama we had at keady, I was taking a vehicle back to change it for another one, which was at Battalion Headquarters. When I got there I had to fix a puncher before I could change the car, I didn't even puncher the fucking thing, so I was well pissed off, I took out the tyre lever and tried to take the tyre off the rim being an angry bastard I pulled so hard the lever slipped off the rim and catapulted right onto my head a quarter of an inch from my right eye, there was blood every where, so now I was even more angry, I had to see the medic and get a few stitches put in. I never bothered with the fucking tyre; I picked up the new car and drove back to Keady. I cooled down on the way back. Sue was pregnant while I was at keady, I put off my leave till she had given birth, we had been sent out to carry out some observation post, we had to sneak into an old farm yard and lie around hidden for twelve hours, radio silence was imposed unless of an emergency, there was some coming and goings which we noted, later I was told that this was one of the IRAs arms cache areas, and later, the guys we saw, were shot dead trying to dig up their weapons. By the time I got back to the police station my boss wanted to see me, while I had been laying around in the farm yard Sue had given Birth to my son "Adam" I waited for a while for the news to sink in, and got two crates of beer for the lads and wet the babies head, in the minging police station of Keady, I went home soon there after to see my new son. I was allowed five days and then I was back again. It was new years eve and my section were on patrol, "Happy fucking New Year" I didn't notice but I should have done but one of my section was acting strange, normally, Mal was chirpy and full of jokes, I put his mood down to New year blues, the patrol went well the town was enjoying the festivities, I was on the way back to the police station having done what we needed to do, Mal suddenly stops in the middle of the road and starts to cry like

A GUARDSMAN'S LOT

a baby, I have to stop the patrol and find out what's wrong with the guy. The rest of the section takes up fire positions in the trees by the side of the road, Mal is now gibbering to me about the anniversary of his fathers death, I said this is not a good time to discuss this we are in the middle of bandit country, and lets talk about it when we get back, he jumps in my face and cocks his rifle and takes the safety off, the fucking gun is pointing strait at me. Now I have to talk to him keep him calm, any thing so long as he didn't pull the trigger, I saw one of my lads who had the GPMG moving slowly round so that he could see what was going on, and shoot the twat if he had to. I don't remember a lot of what I was saying but it was working, the final thing What I do remember saying was:

"Well when you shoot me please go to my new son and tell him why you killed his Daddy" I said

This had the desired effect, his eyes filled and he looked down, quick as a flash I ripped the gun from his hands and smacked him so hard he didn't now were he was, we half carried and half dragged Mal back to the police station, I locked him in a cell, I had to report his actions the man was not well, he left us the next morning. I asked the GPMG man would you have used it on him,

"Yea" "but only after he had slotted you" "he says with a big smile on his face",

"We all laughed". We had to hand over the town of Keady to another regiment, then I was home for two weeks leave, I really needed it. After my leave I returned to the Barracks at Pirbright. So Just to bring you up to date, I was still a Lance Sergeant, more and more responsibility was being given to me, so it was no surprise that on my return to England I was promoted to full Sergeant. Now, in the realms of a Senior Non commissioned officer, a whole New World would soon be bestowed upon me. As a senior NCO there were more opportunities to move into the loan service field. That is to

A GUARDSMAN'S LOT

say postings away from the Battalions and into the real world to see and work with other countries Armies. My next posting was not so glamorous, but it was fun. I was posted to Bovington, the Home of the Royal Armoured Corps, and the old stomping ground of Lawrence of Arabia. I was to be the drill instructor to the Junior Leaders Regiment of the Royal Armoured Corps. I really enjoyed the armoured corps, I had to report for work at Bovington, but there was no married quarter available to move into, so I was given a big caravan as temporary accommodation, I didn't like to move Sue and Adam to the van but needs must. And frankly it wasn't that bad. We were only there for two months, we were getting used to it, I used to call Sue "the gypsy" the wonderful thing about the armoured corps was the mess life, Sue and I had a ball, if I wanted a baby sitter there was always plenty of volunteers, from the boys. My Boss was a Warrant Officer, he was a great guy, we both worked as a team, on parade it was Sir, there after it was first names. Our task was to teach the boys drill and teach the permanent staff to teach drill. It really was a doodle of a job. We moved into married quarters, "Lawrence Close" our next door neighbours had three kids, Wayne, Jane and Shane, it made me laugh when she would call the kids in for tea, it was like she was singing a song. It was when I was at Bovington that we had the real severe snow fall; I had never seen a tank being used as a milk float. The roads to and from work were cleared in no time, and while the rest of Dorset suffered, we were fine. while I was there Sue was pregnant again, which goes to show that I wasn't that busy at work, Emma was born in the hospital at Poole, Dorset, I wanted to go to the birth but Sue didn't want me to leave Adam, I would have probably fainted anyway. At least the next door neighbour baby sat Adam for me when I needed to visit the hospital. After Emma was born I decided that it was time to get the old nuts tied and went and had a vasectomy,

A GUARDSMAN'S LOT

the next day I am back on parade and trying to show no pain, my nuts were the size off watermelons and black as coal, I had to teach the about turn on the march, I got as far as the first movement and my boss sent me home to rest the offending items. The armoured corps at Bovington had a strange ceremony, it was called the tree planting, all new mess members had to buy a tree and it was marched round the barracks and then the owner of the tree would plant it in a pre-prepared hole. The day was finished off with a big shindig in the mess. My tree is still there. my two years flew by I was really happy at Bovington, it was a breath of fresh air in compassion to the Battalion which is where I was to go. So now I find myself driving again to Germany with two kids and Sue, I had my Fathers Triumph 2000 it was a 1965 model which was in mint condition, I paid my Dad £500.00 for it, what a bargain I think he felt sorry for me buying loads of crap cars, but this was great. The drive to Berlin in them days was not so simple, for the final part of the journey your driving down what was called the "corridor" this was West German soil, before the start of the corridor. I had to report to the local RMP post to collect a document that would allow me to drive on west German soil, when you leave the RMP post they give you a time that you should arrive at the other end, this time is précis and if you get there well before the time they (RMP) can nail your arse for speeding, its all to ensure that your kidnapped by the big Red soviet Union, The Russian check point is really quite funny, the letter I had was in English, the Russians would make out that he was reading it, he would hold on to it for about five minutes, then give it back to you, and you would be on your way, this was the only recognised road for British Military "and you had to use it". Except for one of the guys who travelled from the north with his wife and kids and ended up the wrong side of Check Point Charlie, luckily the border guard thought he

A GUARDSMAN'S LOT

was a civvy and stamped their passports, so this guy ended up in big shit with the Army and had to get him and his family new passports. At the time the Battalion were in Berlin, this was before the wall came down, and we were made to be aware of the ever present "red under the bed." On my first day reporting for duty I was duly informed that I was to be the next Sergeants mess caterer for the month. This meant being the full time bar manager, barman, chief glass washer and general dog's body, and all this for no extra pay and the pleasure of not being allowed out of the mess for a month. I should not complain really, as in years gone by, the caterer was required to sleep on a camp bed behind the bar. At least in the late seventies and early eighties we got a room and bed. Mind you the bar would stay open for as long as the Mess members wanted to drink so the bed was not ever worn out. The only thing I can say about being the caterer of one of the most senior Regiments is that there are a lot of piss cats in the Regiment. One such night, I was tending to my duties as bar man, and one of the patrons, was the wife of one of the Company Sergeant Majors, She and her husband had been drinking on and off since lunch time, at 2AM She came to me at the bar and was complaining that I had been watering down the brandy. As she could only taste the coke. Well that was a crock of shit, but I was not going to argue with a drunk, knowing she was drinking Brandy and coke, I took the glass and put in 5 shots of whisky and a drop of coke. That's better she says, the last I see of Mrs Company Sergeant Major that night, is her husband trying to get help to carry her home. She never complained to me again about watering down the drinks. Every morning the "Drill Sergeant" (a Warrant Officer Two) would do a 100% bar and stock check, he would say every day that my stock and cash was down, this of course was always a bag of bollocks, there was no way it could be down unless you were nicking out of the till, I suspect that he

A GUARDSMAN'S LOT

would tell you this just so that you wouldn't nick out of the till, and at the end of the month, your month of Caterer was mentioned at the monthly mess meeting, and the accounts read out, mine was read out and I had made 22% profit for the mess, I also got a vote of thanks from the floor, in the guise of the CSM whose wife was well and truly pissed one night. Officially, we were not allowed out of the mess but I used to sneak home to see the kids when ever I could, it was well known that I went, but most people turned a blind eye, it would have been Barbaric to make a guy stay in the bar for a complete month without a change of scenery. I would never run a pub in my life; the experience of Caterer fucked me for life. I was pleased to get out of there, and was looking forward to a new challenge, so after my month of being put off booze for a year, I was given the grand task, of the mechanised, platoon sergeant, that meant; I was in command of 4 armoured personnel carriers. Two of which, were fitted the "Rarden cannon", "a small anti-tank gun" I am sure I was allotted this task as punishment, the whole lot was just a great big mess, there were thousands of pounds worth of stores missing, not to mention, that we could not account for a missing cannon, only a hundred thousand pounds worth of hardware. When I looked in the stores there was a pile of tools and bits of track, parts of the guns all piled in a big heap in the middle of the floor, the problem being that there was no-one trained or qualified on this bit of kit, so I had to set too with my boys and get it sorted out, we were going to have the Commanding officers inspection in two weeks time, the problem being that I had four weeks work, I ran around the Battalion trying to locate the missing kit, the Quartermaster finally agreed that we had a problem, and told me to indent for the missing stores a bit at a time, so that it wouldn't ring any bells at Army Headquarters, it took over a year but I managed to make up most of the losses, I am sure that the missing cannon was eventually found. Not that I gave a shit, I didn't loose it. Eventually I was saved from this job and another poor mug was found to take it on.

Chapter 14.
Brits verse Yanks.

I was sent to number three Company as the platoon Sergeant of seven platoon, each year in Berlin there is Brigade Competition, and as soon as I arrived at three Company it was time to enter into the inter-platoon competition; this was a big deal, as we had to compete against all the infantry platoons based in Berlin. The whole thing lasted 36 hours we had to march for miles, stop for first aid tests and other military skills; the final competition being the inevitable 3 mile run, assault course and then fire at some targets on the range. Just like the

A GUARDSMAN'S LOT

old Commandants March and Shoot at the Depot, Piece of piss, I hear you say, try it. Then tell me all about it. It was so hard; the weather was down to minus 30, and the cold air burning our lungs as we fought for breath. Near the end, the last quarter of a mile all the REMFS were lined up, screaming for us to get a move on, and come on lads, come where? They all got out of a warm bed, we had spent the last 36 hours either freezing our bollocks off or worst still sweating like pigs, and then when you stop, the sweat turns to ice on your body. So the end is in sight, over the assault course in a dream of pain, then the shooting range, then stop unload. My platoon had not only completed the competition, but fuck me, we had won it! Our reward was a big shield and to be sent down to West Germany, to the American training area and spend two weeks training with the Americans, with one of their infantry battalions at Graffonwier. The British and the Americans had trains that were on a par to the good old "first class" of days gone by, the British train ran during the day and it was nice day out, lunch was provided and you got to see how the West Germans lived, you were not allowed off the train until it had passed through the border, this train went East to West and West to East. The American train travelled South to North and North to South, as it left at night all the carriages were sleepers and dinner was served, then you would get your head down and when you woke up you were in West Germany near to Munich, and then breakfast was served all very civilised, this was our route to Graffonwier, we were met by two great big trucks, they called these "a-dues and a half", because they weighed two and a half tons, we were going to have to learn a whole new version of English. We loaded our kit on to the trucks and climbed aboard, after about an hour we arrive at the training camp it's a huge area, we were accommodated in one large room that could sleep fifty men, and there were fifty in it after we got there, all the ranks sleep in

A GUARDSMAN'S LOT

the same room, so the Platoon Commander was a little put out, I explained to him with a grin on my face "that it would give us the opportunity to get to know one another better"! the whole thing was laid back and the training turned out to be great swan for the boys, who rose to the challenge to (show the fucking yanks what the Guards can do) and show them we did. When the lads saw the cookhouse, they were amazed; us poor Brits eating crap when on exercise, and the Yanks living like kings, Danny went to breakfast on the first day and approached the cook stood by the hot plate.

"How do you want your eggs"? The cook says.

"Preferable, from a chicken, please". "Says Danny".

"No", "I mean how do want it cooked"? Continues the cook.

"Fried", "please". Says Danny in all innocence.

"No", "Sir", "I mean, how do want it fried"? Says the cook getting annoyed.

Danny goes on to explain that he didn't have a fucking clue what the stupid cunt was going on about, until one of the US guys explained.

"Listen", "Buddy" "in the states we can have our eggs fried". Says the Yank, cut short by Danny.

"Yes"! "I know that, I am not fucking stupid". Retorts Danny.

"No" "you're not getting it". The yank says.

"You saying I am thick or what"? shouts Danny.

"No" "not at all" "Sir", stammers the Yank.

"Fuck it" "give me some scrambled eggs". Danny finalizes.

Both the cook and the helpful Yank just stare at Danny in total disbelief.

"Don't mess with these guys"! Says, the Yank.

"Yea", "man", "they want to fight over a goddam egg". Says the cook.

A GUARDSMAN'S LOT

Later I explained to Danny that the Americans have their fried eggs, over-easy, Sunnyside-up, hard, runny or otherwise,

"Fucking hell" "Steve", "I only wanted a bloody fried egg, not a cookery lesson". Says Danny".

"Ok", "Danny" "stick with the scrambled, if it will make it easier for you, I chuckled"

We settled into the daily routine. The Yanks would get up at 0430hrs for breakfast at 0700hrs; we would get up at 0630hrs and still be at breakfast before them. At 0800hrs; each morning I would have my roll call parade, now this was the highlight of the yanks day, they would be fascinated, by our drill, so the guys would put on a bit of a show for our American cousins. I hadn't seen better foot drill even at Buckingham Palace. The yanks would all gather around to watch us. You could hear the "wows" and the "Out-standings" coming from our spectators. After I gave the command to "dismiss" the Yanks would give around of applause, my lads loved it.

Our shooting was better and all of use got our shooting medals, our patrol skills amazed the Americans, this was due to one of my Section Commanders "Danny" it was part of the training to have a inter section "patrol" competition, we saw it as "us" verse "them", the patrol was to be judged by the American umpires, and the type of patrol was to be a recognisance patrol. Which would involve, a lot of belly crawling and real sneaking around, so that you can report on what you see, but enemy must not see you. It was Danny's turn to take his section to Recce an enemy location, which was near the river. It was mid November and the night was black, Danny and the boys set off on their patrol. When they got back some four hours later, the umpires told me:

"Jesus Steve" who are these guys? Says the umpire

Why? I respond, "Were they that bad"?

A GUARDSMAN'S LOT

"Hell no man" the umpire says,

He's telling me that during the patrol, the Americans would take the bridge over the river and then sneak up on the enemy camp and stay hidden for about half an hour and then go back the same route, they were spotted by the enemy crossing the bridge. Danny took his boys down the river bank and they all slide into the water and made their way towards the enemy camp some 400 yards down stream, they crawled towards the enemy camp and watched for over two hours, logging every thing that they saw, there route back was to be different, he took his patrol two miles further down stream, crossed the river and patrolled back to the start line. The umpire was over the moon, I asked him did you go with them,

"Hell no" "the water is to dam cold" "but I watched from a safe distance so as not to compromise their patrol". Said the umpire.

Danny's boys won that competition as well. There was only one real drama, and that involved a couple of my section commanders who got pissed one night, and put a CS gas pellet into one of the ash trays at the all ranks drinking saloon. The outcome is 75 men all trying to clamber out of the building in 2 seconds. It really would not have been a problem but their Commanding officer was there chewing the fat with some politicians from the States. The next morning I made my way over to see him and apologise for my men's behaviour. He could not have been more understanding.

("AH" well, "boys" will be "boys", "says the US boss"

And frankly, the Ares-holes from Washington were getting boring "He said".

I left as if a rocket had been put up my backside. And nothing was ever mentioned again. Our platoon Commander, Tim, was also relieved, as I am sure he saw his career going up in smoke if word had ever got back to Berlin, it never did. Tim was an OK type of guy for an Officer and I know he went on in his career. The

A GUARDSMAN'S LOT

yanks were better for us being there and we did show them, Their Commanders final words to us all was

(Thank God we're all on the same side.) Says the US Commander.

I think these kind words, were due to the fact that he didn't want us to gas him again. Our farewells said to our new friends, and it was back to Berlin and the real world, of more crap and bullshit. The Berlin "crash out" that was our drills to practice if the Russians ever came over the wall, frankly it was a joke, it was anticipated that if the reds were going to attack, our task was to slow them down as much as possible. What a laugh, we used to train at all hours of the day and night. I think the powers that be, were shitting themselves. Should the Russians attack on a Saturday night there would be no one to stop them as half the Berlin Garrison were out of the Barracks getting pissed, or laid, till at least 3AM. Mind you, what I have seen of the Russians then and now I wouldn't have given any worries to the "Shite" we were fed. Just hand over a bottle of Vodka and they are your friends for life, failing which anti freeze will do. Years later I met some ex Russian Army guys in Angola, (no you will not hear that story.)Well not in this book! we all sat and spoke about NATO and the WARSAW PACT, it was very enlightening to say the least. They were more shit scared of their politicians driving the west to war as we were of ours doing the same; I often wonder what would have happened IF? We soon got back into the Battalion routine. The Sergeants Mess was a good place to unwind and it was decided that the Full Sergeants were to have a Regimental dinner night, on the due night we all put on our Mess kits and went to the bar for a couple before dinner, there is always a great atmosphere at these functions, a mini bus was ordered for after the meal and a group of us went on the town, Berlin, was at that time, one city that used to buzz at night, so there we are, twelve Grenadier Sergeants in full bright red Mess dress, going from club to club, we finally ended up in the area around the blue church, in the Kurfursten-Dam, at a club called "Mon Cherie" which was famous for its entertainment, "of and adult nature" after the floor show the whole centre stage would open up to reveal a sunken bath, the size of a hot tub, two girls would grab some unsuspecting member of the audience and strip him, and then he would be invited into the bath, more would happen than was legal, the next guy they invited to have a good scrub was one of our party, Scott was out of his tree, he didn't bother getting undressed he just jumped into the tub, mess kit and all, the girls were not impressed, and we all got thrown out, so Scott is now walking around Berlin dripping wet, complaining that they hadn't even washed his bollocks. We told him to shut the fuck up, we were enjoying ourselves until he disgraced himself. So it was back in the mini bus and finish the night off in the mess, I got home at 0500hrs the next morning, Sue was not impressed, I don't know how Scott got on, he probably blamed us for his Mess kit being ruined.

It was decided that the Battalions in Berlin would provide the umpires for Exercise Crusader, this was too one of the largest mobilisation of man power since D day, so we set off to our allotted tasks, as the unit NBC none commissioned officer it was my task to ensure that when the Enemy declared that they had sent over gas etc: that the troops on the ground being exercised, carried out the correct drills. On this one occasion the lads of a Fusilier Battalion, the lads had it well sorted, and had put on their gas masks, I went to where their Company Commander was, no not this clown, sat in his tent drinking tea, no gas mask on. "Sorry" "Sir", I said, but your 2i/c will have to take over, Your dead, I said

You have just been gassed. I smiled as I said it

A GUARDSMAN'S LOT

He was still bitching when the head umpire arrived, I don't know what was said but the wanker of a Company Commander, slid out of his tent looking very sheepish. This was really a steady job, when we were not required we could always be found at some local beer drinking house, within a short while of pouring beers down our neck and buying for the locals we could all speak perfect German and the locals could speak perfect English, "well not really" but we managed to understand each other very well, a drunk is the same in any language. We returned to Berlin all of us with similar stories, of fucking the officers around but not the guys. I was given a new Officer to break in (Platoon Commander), he was a ex "spotty" little public school boy, he arrived at the Company thinking he was going to inspect the platoon, he was dirty ill shaven and to top it all had his carpet slippers on. I went up to him and suggested that he should go back to the Officers Mess, and get himself sorted out and cleaned up prior to coming back to inspect my Platoon, he was most put out,

"you": you": "can not talk to me like that", "I am an officer": he says.

"might I suggest you act like one", "Sir", I responded.

He left me and went into see the Rock. "the Company Commander" a very hard old school Officer, the little lad was only in his office for thirty second's, and was in tears when he left. "Bless him" one day my mate Steve told me that he had been selected to go to Uganda, lucky bastard I said, he was the CQMS of the Company, so he was given leave prior to going off on his new mission. That meant that I had to take over his job, so I moved to my "Stores" (blanket stacking) days I was the acting CQMS, but only as a Sergeant, the Company went on exercise and my job was to ensure that the boys were fed and watered, I had a cook attached to the Company to do the cooking, "Gordon" had left years ago, so we had a proper cook, who new what he was doing. If, as the CQMS, you could not hack it in the field, then your career was going to be very limited, and you would not survive. The job is very important, as the CQMS its your task to ensure that no matter where your Company is you have to be able to re-supply them day or night, food-petrol-ammunition, and any thing else that they might need. And it is no good if you cannot read a map, I've known so many guys, that have driven around for hours because they couldn't find their guys, and then when he does find them the food is cold and the vehicles have run out of fuel, not good for moral, I found that I took to this like a duck to water, nothing was ever a problem, if the boss wanted it the boss got it, I had a team of two store men to help me, who were by far the hardest workers I had seen in a long time, the boys were getting real picky and were making a joke to me that they would love a nice meat or apple pie, so I waited till they went out for the daily exercise, and got hold of the cook and we made a "pug oven" this is a pile of bricks put on the top of the frame, that is over the number one burner "cooker", the bricks are laid in such away as to look like a pizza oven, then the whole outside is covered with mud to keep the heat inside the bricks, a metal shelf is fixed into the oven and another piece of metal is used for the door. That day the cook is making pastry and cooking beef out of tins, peeling onions, the farmer of the farm we were staying at "in his barns and out buildings" had a huge pile of apples, so we raided the pile and set to peeling apples, the store-men were into this by now and wanted to help, so they were handed knives and told to start peeling apples, the apples were put into a big "Dixie" (large pan) and boiled the apples, the boys were due back at about 1800hrs and supper was to served at 1830hrs, time was not on our side, the cook had to time the use of the oven to the last possible minuet, he didn't want to burn the crusts of the pies, its really difficult to control the heat of the oven, there is no up or down knob to control the heat. All the preparations were ready, and just to finish the effect we got all the tables we could find and laid them out in the courtyard of the farm, the farmers wife kindly loaned us some white cloth and so table cloths were placed on the table, by the time we finished the court yard could have been a garden café in Paris, and just to top it off I wrote the menu on the Black board and placed it by the serving tables. The menu was:

MENU: CAFÉ ALA COMPANY TRES

Steak pie, with short crust pastry.
Mashed, creamed potatoes.
Glazed, Carrots.
Gravy, ala barn.
With bread and butter, if required.

AND ON THE SWEET TROLLEY

STEVE RUDGE

Baked apple pie in short crust pastry.
Fresh, milk custard, ala farm.

With Tea ala chef to follow.

The time was moving on the boys arrive back and went into the barn that was their accommodation which was the opposite to where we were, the Company Commander (The Rock) came round for a chat, he saw what we had done and was over the moon, he said,

"I don't care if its all burnt the boys will love it." he says

The boys arrived with their mess tins, knives, forks and spoons, complete with black plastic mugs, they saw the results of our hard work, and it went down well, the menu was received with great laughs from the guys, now all we had to do was to make sure the food matched the mood, the poor cook is sweating his bollocks off, I really must have placed him under real pressure, out comes the first pie, perfect, crisp

A GUARDSMAN'S LOT

and lightly browned, the rest is history the lads enjoyed their Supper and I must admit the cook and the store men were heroes for ever. When we got back from the exercise the boss called me into the office and told me that I was to be promoted to "Colour Sergeant" all my hard work had paid off. Now I was A colour Sergeant and the battalion would be moving back to England the kids were getting older and sue and I it would be better to buy a house and allow the kids a stable education, so we purchased a house in Grantham in Lincolnshire. When it was time to return from Berlin to England Sue went strait to Grantham and we set up the new house, I was on leave for a while and helped with the un-packing and putting strait, I even put up a bath room shelf, that was a big deal for me, I was and still am the worst DIY man alive.

Chapter 15.
Africa Calling.

Once I got back to the battalion, which had moved to Hounslow in Middlesex, I was asked to go to Uganda, all this time and Steve still hadn't gone, so I had to move to Pirbright to get ready for the rest of the team to arrive. Here we got together with rest of the team and conducted some pre tour training, getting to know other weapons and brushing up on our fitness.

Thank God for Africa and our great British Commonwealth, there is always some shit-hole country that needs our help, and good old Mr Milton Obote of Uganda was no exception. By

A GUARDSMAN'S LOT

1982/83, his Liberation Army, was running amok in Uganda, killing all that came in their path, considering that they had not been paid for over 6 months, the soldiers were somewhat pissed off. Consequently the Government of the day needed some help to sort it out, subsequently the Commonwealth Training team to Uganda was formed, most commonwealth countries sent a few troops over, but the British sent the most manpower, there were approximately 15 Brits and the rest of the team were from the other countries, Johnny Clavering Scots Guards Commanded this out post in the middle of East Africa. If it wasn't so serious it would be funny that of the mentality in Africa, the common person has nothing, the politicians have it all, and it is the same today. And the stupid rich nations of the world keep pumping billions of dollars into these African countries so it goes from one rich country to a numbered Swiss bank account for the ministers of the African country, and the people it's intended to help, "get," "fuck all".

After a couple of weeks getting ourselves sorted out at Pirbright and getting the team together, our flight tickets were issued British Airways to "Entebbe" Uganda. We set off to go to Gatwick Airport, we get there and are told to go to Stanstead Airport, never mind these things happen, so we arrive at Stanstead, and find out that our tickets are really for "Ugandan Airways", we check in, and hand over the box that I am carrying with 10 Browning 9mm Pistols, these go with the pilot and will be given to me at customs when we get there. We have to board the plane, When I get on the aircraft only a quarter of the plane has got seats, and there grotty, I look behind the ripped curtain dividing the aircraft from the seats, to see what's on the other side of our seats, its full of boxes and cargo, the presidents private shopping no-doubt. Never mind, the government pays top pound for BA prices and we sit in shit. And it gets worse; the

Airports drinks supply guy arrives and wants to hand over the drinks to the steward.

"Payment first please in cash"! "Says the drinks guy"

"I am not" "having enough Money", Says the Ugandan steward.

"OK" "no drinks" says the drinks guy.

We are all listening to this, and I know just what the guys are thinking, and are getting a little wanked off sitting in a shit fucking aircraft and no fucking drinks.

"Can you help me" "Sir", says the steward to me.

"What the fuck do want me to do buy the fucking drinks for you" I say"

"Yes please" "I am paying you back after I am selling the drinks", the steward grins at me.

Now I must be fucking really dim, but excuse me, I buy the whole trolley of drinks at cost, from the airports drinks Guy and then I have to buy a can of beer for the staggering price of

£1.00 a can from the steward. who has not even paid for the fucking stuff.

"Fuck off" I say

By now the rest of the boys are ragging me and calling me a tight cunt.

"Fuck you" , "you buy the fucking drinks" I say to the boys

"Sorry mate but I have to go" Says the airports drinks guy, and starts to Manoeuvre the trolley off the plane.

"I am giving you free drinks all of the flight" "Sir", the steward pleads to me.

"OK" "how much"? I say to the airports drink guy.

"Thirty five pounds" "mate" he says

I hand over the money and calm is restored, I couldn't help but feel that I had been stitched up, I did get my money back, some where over the Sahara desert, and I did get my free drinks. Problem was the fucking beer was warm. The rest of the flight from London to Entebbe was fine, we landed and went through to the customs,

A GUARDSMAN'S LOT

now here was a problem, we were not in uniform and we also had to collect the box containing our hand guns, the customs were getting really excited, and would not let the weapons through, I took control of the situation, and 5 brand new one pound notes later and we were on our way, guns, and all. Welcome to Africa. Our mission was to train and discipline an army that had not seen fresh meat for months, or been paid for months, and lived on boiled beans. Well at least we had 3 square meals a day. Thanks to Johnny's superb leadership skills and planning, and not forgetting the hundreds of thousands of pounds donated by the Governments of the commonwealth. There were many parts of this task that really were not to amusing so I will move onto the bits that were. Our students were civil war veterans not used to any real type of Military Discipline or the Geneva Convention. They arrived at our camp at Jinja, for their training, dressed in rags, we fitted them out with what uniforms could be had, the accommodation was poor but better than the bush. The test case students were lined up for inspection, I walked up and down the line and all their faces had at least a months growth of hair, I instructed them to report to the Quartermaster and get a razor and to be shaved the next time I see them. Well, the next day they were lined up again, this time their faces looked like a wild cat had slashed them all. I asked what had happened? I was informed that the Quartermaster had issued razor blades but no razor, and that the students had tried to shave with just the blade, stupid or dedication, I would never know. They were given razors the next day; the Quartermaster was thinking he could sell them at the market. What an areshole. The General from the Ministry of Defence came to visit one day, so in true Regimental fashion, we organised a Regimental dinner night. My task was to ensure the food and staff were doing what and when it should happen, all was going to plan until the speeches, at which the Jamaican contingent and Sierra Leone guys kept disappearing, one at a time and then Reappearing. I was trying for ages to track down the temporary waitress to ensure the drinks kept coming, but to no avail, so I gave up on that one. A few days later the Canadian medic tells us at breakfast, that the girl we used the other night to wait on at the dinner, had been to see the doctor, with what appeared to be syphilis, there was a clatter of knives and forks and five of the guys, who only two minutes earlier had been enjoying a hearty meal, all left the dinning room, looking very sheepish. The sick parade that night was well attended. It transpired that they were sneaking out for a quick one, then telling their mates who would follow on. All's well that ends well it was only yeast build up, some lucky horny guys could relax again. I don't think there was any after dinner jokes that night. One Saturday night we had some visitors who had brought some young white ladies with them, needless to say there was an over abundance of sniffing going on, however one of the girls wanted to play charades, well who were we to deny that. So, 12 hairy arsed tough soldiers, prancing about like school kids, Des from the Royal Tank Regiment, was up doing his silent animations, when all of a sudden, the night calm was shattered by heavy gun fire in our direction. We all bugged out to retrieve our weapons, there was a funny side to it all, Des was still bitching that he was winning and wanted his turn again, Des was told to fuck off and get a life. In words of one syllable. Not forgetting the girls, they must have been the most protected ladies ever. Not one of the super heroes that night got any, after the fire fight, the visitors and girls went back to Kampala. Des was still going on for days, wanting his turn again. The Madervarny family had a huge plantation just outside Jinja, it was run down through years of war, so they had returned from the UK to pick up where they left off, after Idi Amin had thrown them out. We were invited to go over and take some rest time

A GUARDSMAN'S LOT

and relax. There was a huge reservoir full of green brackish water, Bully from Jamaica went for a swim, in minutes he is screaming, "get it off me" poor Bully had a leach attached to his left bollock, no one volunteered to remove it. We had to travel every month to Nairobi for the rations, a three-day round trip. The journey was boring and long, at one stretch of the road the baboons would come hopping to the forest edge and flash their arses in the air to us. Ronnie pulled his pistol out and fired a couple of wild shots in their direction missing of course, but what he didn't think about was the empty cases flying around the cab I nearly drove the truck into the ditch, dodging the dam things. Over all the training of the Army went well, we must have done something right, because when I returned much later in life which was in 1997 I went up to Uganda and while I was there I bumped into one of my old students, who is now the head of internal security for the present Government, there was still that respect offered, as from student to teacher, and he still remembered me, that night a lot of memories and a few more pints were put to rest. Back to 1983 It was during this time in Uganda that the Falklands started, all we wanted to do was get back so we could do our bit, we had to stay. Our thoughts and feelings for the lads who went south were ever present.

At this time, and still today, the young men at sixteen in Uganda still get circumcised, this is a big deal, and we were invited by the cook to his sons circumcision, so a load of us went over to his village, well, talk about an eye opener. This poor lad was striped naked, with white paint all over his body and a white sheet, he appeared to be drugged. Mind you if someone was going to rip my foreskin off I think I would be well drugged as well. So the young man stands there and the head honcho takes a rusty looking knife, pulls the young mans foreskin out about 3 inches and proceeds to hack away, we were all hard men, but you could see the inner wincing of all concerned. Two weeks later the cook is asking for help for his son. The poor young bastard ended up with blood poisoning and had it not been for the help of our medical team the poor kid would now be dead. My tour of duty over the six months went quickly, and I would have liked to have stayed, but we had to let others have there chance to change the world.

On my return to the UK after a spot of leave, the battalion was in Canada doing some more training, the R&R (rest and recuperation) was every man could do what he wanted, the main attraction was the Rocky Mountains, now in the new world you can not hire a car without a major credit card, however there was one little hire shop that would take the MOD form 90 (army ID card) and cash. So the standing joke was: MOD form 90? Thank you Sir that will do nicely, in reference to the American Express advertising slogan. At the end of the final exercise some bright spark (officer of course) thought it would be a super idea to do some cleaning up, that meant picking up the rubbish from the live firing range. This was a disaster waiting to happen, as the whole of the British army used this area to fire live ammunition mortar bombs etc: the Company were half way through the clean up, and someone must have kicked the tail fin of a 81mm Mortar bomb, BANG, and in less than a second 15 guys were seriously hurt, what a good idea it was to clean the range.!!!! Fucking twit of an Officer. After this saga we returned to UK and I found myself posted again. It was around about this time that things in my personal life were not going so good, I had left Sue and was living in the Sergeants Mess, I would try and see the kids as often as I could but the marriage was falling apart.

I was posted to Shornecliffe near Folkestone as a CQMS. I move my kit into the Sergeants mess, like a small hotel except I had to Clean my own room, not that, that was a big deal. So

A GUARDSMAN'S LOT

Monday nights it was down town to the local grab a granny and act like the oldest swinger in town. It was really all good clean fun. It was while I was Shornecliffe that I was summoned to London to my Regimental Headquarters, to, "discuss my Private life" to me this was a complete bag of bollocks, what the fuck did it have to do with some gobshite Colonel, the fact that I was going to get a divorce. The conversation went like this. The Colonel said:

"Well Colour Sergeant", "what's this I hear about you and your wife"

(Silent pause) I was fucked if I was going to make it easy for him to push his dirty little nose into my private life.

He continued:

"You realise that this could reflect very badly on your career"? He said.

(Another pause) so now not only do I have to live breath and shit army, I am expected to love who they fucking tell me to, my temper was starting to get the better of me. The Colonel continues:

"You know we are all like a family we have to look after each other", "So what do have to say about it Colour Sergeant"?

I stood there thinking: that I should tell this clown to just fuck off and mind his own business, what the hell did he now? And all this family crap, where was he when my bills came in? It was just a crock of shit. All I did say was.

"If you wish to discuss my divorce then would he please direct it to my solicitor".

I think he must have been shocked as this time it was his turn to be silent, I could just imagine his thoughts: What, how dare this little grub not talk to me, who does he think he is, well, what do I say now? As there is nothing in Queen's rules and regulations that can make him discuss it. I helped him out by saying:

"Sir", if my private life ever effects my professional life then I would be obliged if you would please tell me".

A GUARDSMAN'S LOT

I was asked to leave his office, and that was that, or so I thought. I was still steaming, I was muttering under my breath, nosey bastard dragging me all the way to London for fuck all. I did reflect on this some years later, when I was told that the same Colonel who spoke to me that day, was due to retire in the late nineteen eighties, and that the day after he had retired, he dumped his wife and ran off with a younger bit of stuff, and that his wife was totally unaware of any thing going on, so this fucking guy was not only a nosy bastard but a bloody hypocrite to boot. Don't you just love the Officer Corps?

Well it made me laugh. The fact that I had really thumbed my nose at the Regiment did not do me any good, but in retrospect it gave me a lot more chances than most, as I will explain. I stayed at Shornecliffe for about 18 months and just got on with my job, there is not a lot to say about this posting other than an interlude in my life. Counting blankets.

By now I was well known in the Ministry of Defence within the loan Service division, these are the guys who send people like myself all over the world doing strange little jobs for foreign Governments, like Uganda. For some strange reason there are not many people who volunteer for such jobs, me, I loved it, without sounding big headed I was well qualified by this time in all aspects of Military Skills, my instructional skills were excellent and still are today.

Chapter 16.
The Sun Beckons.

When I received a call from the MOD asking if I wanted to go to Saudi Arabia, I jumped at the chance. In the mid eighties during one of the many Hajj pilgrimages to Mecca, the Shiite Moslems had caused major problems by barricading them-selves in the catacomb's at Mecca, The Saudi National Guard had tried to get them out, but with no luck, so what they did was just to blow the whole fucking lot up men and catacombs together. This did not really go down to well within the Moslem world. The Saudi Government requested help from the

British Government to train their National Guard in the art of internal security, crowd control and counter insurgency. Hence the phones call to me.

Well I did not need much time to think about it,

"Yes please Sir", "when do I go"? I said

"Not just yet", from the MOD.

Within two weeks I was summoned again to London to discuss the Saudi Mission. We met at an office block near to Liverpool street station; this was where I would meet my fellow team members. I was expected, and was shown into a suite of richly furnished offices, six other guys were there just making small talk. We did the normal introductions, so as not to offend I will not use the teams real names, we will call one Jock, Paddy, and Taffy, strangely enough the countries of origin were Scotland, Ireland, and Wales, so I am not straying to far from real names. The other three guys present, one was to be our boss there, a Lieutenant Colonel who

A GUARDSMAN'S LOT

was a bit of a dip stick, as time would prove, the other two introduced themselves as coming from some Company or other, I really do not remember the name given. My own point of view was that they were from one of the many little organisations that really do not exist, but with full Government financing. The main topic of conversation here was to get the Saudis to buy British if the opportunity ever rose its self. This I found to be a very strange request, for a start it was not down to us, to worry about the trade and industry of Great Britain. We were going they're to do a job, and that was that, the thought crossed my mind that maybe the Dipstick was on commission. After we had finished with the sell Britain guys, it was the turn of the boss to talk, well, what had I let myself into, he was talking out of his arse hole, between us, the four instructors had over 45 years of instructional experience. The boss was talking crap in regards to lesson plans and how we should be teaching the Saudi National

Guard, the four of us looked at each other, you could see on the teams faces the same look of pending doom, after the boss had gone out of the room, we all looked at each other. As if by Que. We all burst into loud laughter,

"He sounds like a right fucking dick" , says paddy

Jock was to busy pissing his self laughing, and Taffy was just saying:

"Well boy's" "this is going to be fun". Says taffy

My comments were in tune with the guys, and really the boss was a total dick head. Myself and the rest of the team sorted out what needed to be done and over the next couple of weeks we were getting to know each other, I sorted out some accommodation at Shornecliffe for the guys and we set too, preparing for the lessons we would need to teach. There was a lot to brush up on. While we were busying ourselves our passports had to go off to the Saudi Embassy, it was nice to see that when we got them back

A GUARDSMAN'S LOT

they had given us Diplomatic status. When work was done the married guys would try and get away home for the weekends, as we would be away for a minimum of six months. By mid August we were ready to roll, armed with our air tickets via Saudi Air and our tropical uniforms packed in our suitcases, we were off. At Heathrow, we had, what, we thought would be our last alcohol for six months, little did I know. Paddy was moaning about the fact that: "Here we are with fucking Diplomatic Stamps and the cheap shit ragheads fly us cattle class." It was funny really, but it is a well-known fact that you can put a Squaddie in a Rolls Royce and he would bitch that the fucking clock was ticking to loudly. Once boarded on the flight, I looked around at our fellow passengers all in their Savill Row suits and the ladies in the latest Paris fashions. The 747 took off and we were on the way, visions of "Lawrence". It didn't take me long to crash out and sleep till dinner, rice and chicken, no alcohol was being served so that was jock well pissed off. After dinner I nodded off again, by the time I woke up we were on the final approach for Riyadh International Airport. I needed badly to take a piss, looking round the aircraft the lines were to long, I just had to nip it for a while, I did notice that the Savill Row suits had been exchanged for the standard white robes with matching head gear and that the ladies were all in black with their faces all covered. Had the plane crashed Through a time warp. I finally got to piss as the wheels were being lowered, and some faggot steward banging on the door, asking:

"Could you please hurry", says the steward.

"Sorry mate", "I got to piss", I shouted through the door.

I was intent on enjoying it. Apart from which, I was busy off loading the entire after-shave and deodorants into my pockets. The 747 touched down and we disembarked, you could see the instant wealth hit you in the face, marble floors and walls, the local Arabs doing sweet fuck all

A GUARDSMAN'S LOT

and all the imported workers, running round like coolie's. This was to be "situation normal" as we would soon find out. I really must admit that the first impressions were of a fabulous looking Airport, and I have seen a lot in my life. Once through customs the boss met us and we were whisked away in the Range Rover. The drive to Riyadh took us about an hour; it was amazing to see the buildings rising out of the desert, the sheer splendour of it all, it screamed of money and more money. Every other street corner had some new building going up on the desert floor, it was one big building site, Taffy said: we will find ourselves in some shit hole, like what I was in, when I was in Spain on holiday. How wrong, could he have been? The Range Rover pulled up outside this hotel, The Riyadh Palace Hotel, a couple of guys dressed like the Sheikh of Arabie ran to open doors and the luggage disappeared, Paddy was already talking to the guys, his Arabic was quite good, mine was to get better. Stepping inside it was like walking into an air-conditioned Sultans Palace, marble floors carpets that would sell for ten thousand pounds a throw. Jock and myself were discussing ways of relieving them of the carpets and flogging them in London. We still never came up with a plan, apart from which I wasn't going to get my hand cut off, for some pretty looking carpets. As I sat in the leather sofa I sank so far into it I thought I had gone down to hell. The boss had us all checked in, and a meeting was called, we sat around and were told to be ready the next morning for 0700 hours, in uniform, at that the boss fucked off. Well he had to he was over in Saudi for two years, so his wife was there, and as we were to find out she was the Boss in their house. Left to our own devices we made our way to our allotted rooms the bags were there, my room was a double very nice, well it had to be, this five star hotel was to be home for the next six months. We were told that all expenses will be covered, what a great bunch these Arabs are. I took a shower and

A GUARDSMAN'S LOT

got dressed and went on a recognisance of my domain. The night air was cool; it was a lovely looking Hotel with swimming pool, gym, sauna and all the necessary tools for the top executive businessman. I was looking at a menu for one of the two restaurants, one, which was open 24 hours a day, I was joined by Paddy and we sat about and talked shite for awhile. At some time we said good night to each other, and I went to bed. In the room, on the bedside locker was an arrow glued to the top, and Mecca written under it, I asked Paddy the next morning, in regards to the arrow..

"They need to know that their facing Mecca" "when they pray", "as Allah, does not take to kindly to rag heads, who moon him four times a day", he said:

It made perfect sense to me, so it was agreed that the arrows would be turned around as soon as we got some glue. So there we were waiting for the boss, who turned up over an hour late, no apologising or fuck all. You could have cut the air with a knife. We, were three highly trained, motivated and professional Warrant Officers and one young keen Captain, the worst thing you can do to a team of men like us, is to treat us with no respect, as the boss had just done. Which he would live to regret?

"What" an arrogant cunt: said jock, who just stood up and walked away, the boss missed his comment. but asked

"Where he going", the boss said.

"He's been waiting for over an hour to take a shit, so now he's getting one". I said.

It went right over the boss's head.

"Right chaps" "who's for coffee"?, the boss squeaked,

"No thanks", we said

We would no more drink coffee with this clown, than share our blood with a vampire. He had really pissed us off. It was starting to dawn on us, as to why a Lieutenant Colonel in the British Army was posted out of his regiment, well away from England, in some made up job,

A GUARDSMAN'S LOT

that a 10 year old could do with his cock in his hand. The man was a total fucking buffoon, this job was well out of his league, and he knew it, but being to arrogant he was going to fuck it up, then blame everyone else, I have seen it many times. Promote a guy up and get rid of him, the boss was a typical example of this, god help us! We sat around listing to how the boss wanted the training to be conducted, he wanted us to teach all the lessons first, then get our students to teach them, I tried to explain to him that we are training them to become instructors, and that each lesson should be taught by us, then they should go away and with their lesson plans of that one lesson, then come back and teach it, and that the students should all teach the lesson. Not as he wanted, by the time it was their turn to teach lesson one, they would have forgotten it. That way the students are not waiting 3 months before getting into the teaching mode. Suffice it to say he was already fucking it up. Any arguments fell on deaf ears.

"OK" we will do it your way" I said.

Even Taffy the Captain agreed, the boss was being stupid, generally the Officer corps sticks together but even this was not the case. And this was only the 2nd day in country. We had to wait a couple more days for the Saudis to arrange for the interpreters, but it gave us time to go to the National Guard headquarters and see the top man, the kings Brother, a very nice well educated guy. We had to observe the usual rituals of tea and small talk, before business, I was getting a good taste for mint tea. Then it was off to the training area, which was their barracks, the camp was a good hours drive away from the hotel, and a barracks is a barracks is a barracks, and soldiers are the same the world over. We did our survey of where we would take our lessons etc: we talked to the students and generally just milled around, something we would be experts at after six months. Screw this I said lets fuck off back to the hotel and sample the pool, no one complained so off we went. A light lunch followed by a swim and we were ready for the next pile of shit to be dumped on our heads. It came that night, the boss appeared and informed us that two of the team was to go to Jeddah, to train the guys there. Taffy and Paddy were detailed off to go, and that was that. I have not seen them since they left the very next day. We did talk on the phone to compare notes. The boss was becoming somewhat of a standing joke, not only with us but the Saudis, who treated him with kindness believing that they would not get to heaven if they were to hurt the inflicted one. "They do have a way with their language." It was time to get down to the task in hand. We went about our teaching lessons, with the knowing dread that we were really pissing into the wind, the boss wanted it done this way so he got it that way, the up shot being that the first six weeks were totally wasted, so I will move on, he never did admit his failings, but we were left to it and he fucked off to Cyprus on holiday, that suited us fine. Jock and myself were making good progress, then the shit head arrived back and started to interfere yet again,

"Yes Sir",

"No Sir",

"Three bags full Sir",

And as soon as he went,

Fuck you to Sir",

And we carried on teaching the way it should be done. Sadly we were now 6 weeks behind schedule and had to start from scratch.

Half way through was their holy month of Ramadan, and between sun rise and sun set nothing gets done in the Arab world, so that was us totally unemployed for a month. I do not know how Jock passed his time but the swimming pool took a hammering. By this time I had met Patricia from the United States, who worked at the King Kalid Hospital, on one of my many trips to donate a pint of blood, at £60.00 a pint I was walking round like an anaemic rat. I used two Hospitals one every month, so, as

A GUARDSMAN'S LOT

all expenses at the hotel were on the house, the 60 quid was pocket money, so my wages were never touched, being in Saudi, roughing it, I was also on loan service pay, that increased my salary to double the norm, all to be saved in the UK, "lovely jubbly" so when I wasn't busy with Patricia I was being a lazy blood donating swimmer of the year, getting bronzed by the pool. One day Patricia and I went to one of the many ex-patriot compounds, to meet some of the American community, it was to be a two day party, some fucking party was my complaint prior to going, no booze.

"Don't worry Honey" was all Patsy would say.

We got there and the big steel gates were closed, parked the car, and met our hosts, I was handed a glass of red wine, which tasted like shit, I said nothing. I asked

"How's it was made"?

"Gee whiz man", "we go to the supermarket, buy 5 gallons of grape juice and 20 pounds of sugar, put it all together and leave it sealed for a couple of weeks, and the Saudi heat does the rest" Chuck told me.

Well, after the first three glasses who gave a shit how it was made, It was doing the job fine, thank you. One of the guys there worked for some aircraft corporation, who just happened to have been an ex county and western fiddle player who used to play for the Grand Old Opera, in Nashville, he was fired from the band, not due to his lack of talent, but because he was an alcoholic and failed to make it on time. The more pissed we got the better the guy played. In between renditions of the Devil came down to Georgia, his only words were,

"Give me another slug" "of that mule piss with the foam farted off"

I think apart from being a fine fiddle player, he was a fucking good wine critic as well. The party was over and we had to stay the night, I didn't want to spend time in nick and get flogged for being drunk. In the morning I dropped

A GUARDSMAN'S LOT

Patricia off at work and went back to the hotel, for another swim.

On the road to the barracks, the locals would drive like men possessed, at the turning to the Barracks, a large sleeping police man was put over the main road, this lump of tarmac was put into place over night. Someone's idea of a joke. The cars would scream along the road at speeds that would make Nigel Mansell look slow. By the time that they saw the hump it was too late, the cars were airborne, sailing into the surrounding desert, totally written off; many a lost life, finally a warning sign was erected. The area around the hump looked like "Jacks Scrap Yard" I must admit to leaving half an inch of rubber on the road the first time I encountered the killer hump. On the subject of motor accidents, poor old Jock was driving in town one day, and one of the locals drove into him. Jock was arrested, the logic behind this: even though it was not his fault, was, that as an "infidel" had Jock not been in Saudi then the accident would not have occurred. Jock phoned me at the hotel to say

I am stuck in some shitty stinking cell, jock says. and that the inmates are eyeing my arse up, and please, fucking do something to get me out, continued jock.

Best you practice safe sex and ensure a condom is to worn. I said.

He did not see this as very funny, well not at the time anyway. I ended up having a fucking big argument with the boss, who's comments like:

"We can not rock the boat Sergeant Major", says the boss.

"Do something" "you gutless wonder or I will". I said

"And what will you do Sergeant Major"? He says

I hung up the phone, I immediately phoned one of my students who was the cousin to the prince, within 15 minutes Jock was on the phone saying:

A GUARDSMAN'S LOT

"Come on then you cunt come and get me".

Jock was out, and no thanks to our spineless leader. The only time I recall the boss doing anything right was when we had to get the training on film, the boss was running round like Steven Spielberg trying to cover all the shots and angles, when the final cut was shown I had to admit it was quite good, Jock suggested that:

"Why doesn't the Areshole fuck off to Hollywood" says jock

"It would be better for all concerned", "except the movie moguls may like him", "and make him a millionaire" Continues Jock.

On one of our last Fridays we were told that there was to be a public execution in chop, chop square. Without further prompting we were on our way, the whole of Riyadh must have been there to see it. Apparently some mangy little Yemeni had raped a couple of young boys, and being a dirt poor looser, had no money to pay blood money, so his fate was settled. Afternoon prayers, the tension in the square starts to build up, finally the big door slams open, the target of hate is held up between two burly guards, the victim looks half dead, it was suggested that he looks like a good guardsman after a good Saturday night out. There is no fucking around, the holy man says a few words, may Allah have mercy on his soul etc: all is lost on the crowd baying for blood. The bloke is there his knees are kicked so he folds like a drunk to his knees, his head is pushed down, and in less than a second the huge Arab executioner has dropped the scimitar down, its supposed to be over in one chop, I gather the executioner had a disliking to Yemenis, who rape young boys. It took him two chops to finalise the act. The crowd loved it,

"This is one way to stop all the crap" I said to Jock.

"Yea" says Jock.

"Well, mate, back to the hotel and some lunch" I said.?

A GUARDSMAN'S LOT

"Not just yet Steve" "Feeling a bit sick", he says,

"Maybe later". Jock says

Fuck the little shit he got what he deserved. A little of Arab law should be used on the youth of Britain, who think its fun to kill- rape and generally behave like animals. Seeing the blood gush 10 feet across the road would let the little fuckers think twice, it opened my eyes.

Coming to the end of our tour the students had intimated that the King was going to thank us personnel for a job that he thought was well done? Who were we to disagree with the King. The normal practice at that time was: if you got to see the king, he would reward you with a gold Rolex watch with his face on it. It was a few days later that we heard the truth. The two faced Lieutenant Colonel had said not to bother with the chaps as they were only doing their jobs, There was no consoling Jock, he wanted to kill the bastard. I must agree that a $20.000 watch would have been a nice way to say thanks. But of course the boss already had his one. I had the opportunity to see the bribe system first hand. It was also my job to evaluate the new anti riot equipment that was pouring in from all the countries in the modern world. The Saudi Government would not cut any corners or worry about cost. One night during the evaluation week, a knock was received on my door, outside stood a little man in a cheap suit, his words today are still in my mind.

"If you make sure they buy anything made by company X you will get one percent of the value paid into your bank in England" he said

"Get the fuck out of here" I said to him.

I could kick myself today, as the final orders placed were well over $3,000.000. 00. But I still had integrity. What makes me think, is, was the boss taking kick backs, as there was a lot of British made junk in use by the National Guard? We will never know, but I remember the comment: "We can not make waves".

A GUARDSMAN'S LOT

WHY I WONDER? The final lesson that we had to teach the Saudi National Guard was how to blow things up properly. So a Land Rover was used on this demonstration, with only one pound of Plastic explosive we sent the Rover flying over the desert. My final comment to the lads were:

"Next time you have shit at Mecca" I said.

"You will know just how much explosive is required to blow the Shiite's to hell". I said

They thought it was funny. It was time to report to the boss and have our reports issued on how he believed our performance had gone over the last 6 months. It was no shock to any of us that he thought we were not fit to shovel shit. The report that he had written on me, was thrown back on his desk, and I told him, that in my opinion: he was not a fit enough officer, to report on a Harrods doorman, let alone a Senior Warrant Officer, in the most senior infantry Regiment in the British Army, he was gobsmacked, even more so when I took the report and tore it in two, threw it on his desk and said have a nice day, saluted and marched straight into his boss, the Brigadier, who told me not to worry, I said I wasn't worried just so angry that idiots like him really believe their own bullshit. Cut a long story short the brigadier wrote my report again personally, and then told the idiot boss to sign it or pack up and fly home to England, the money grabbing cunt signed it. On return to the UK I went on leave for a couple of weeks

Chapter 17.
How Life Turns.

After my leave I rejoined the Battalion at Hounslow, Calvary Barracks, what a total shit hole this place was, the guys were sleeping in the converted stables, the whole place was falling apart. I took over as The Company Sergeant Major of Support Company. It was back to the same old storey of Public duties, Royal guards, this time for me it wasn't so bad being a Warrant Officer and all. Patricia and I were still corresponding, and it seemed a good idea to get married. I managed to get an RAF flight to Washington DC for the huge price of £12.00

return, from there I got the cheapest flight to Atlanta, Patricia met me there, after a night in a motel, we drove to Huntsville, Alabama. Then it was all go to get the blood tests and licence, our honeymoon was spent at her Daughters house, that first night we all went out to some Red Neck bar, Patricia was so proud of her new husband that: she announced to the whole bar:

"My Steve is so tough he can lick anyone in the house,"

I could have shrunk up my arse hole, luckily no one took up her challenge, she got a good talking to that night. And other things. We drove up to Saginaw Michigan to meet the folks, that was OK her Sister was a bit weird, she drove around in a bloody big pink Cadillac. Generally they were all nice guys and made me feel at home. I returned to England to get some accommodation sorted out for us. Then She joined me. From day one of her arriving she did nothing but bitch. If it wasn't the weather, it was the fact that I had to attend

A GUARDSMAN'S LOT

the Mess meetings. She didn't drink so we were all seen to be raving alcoholics, so what, I hear you say, well after a while the bitching wears you down. So it was a pleasure to go off training again, this time to Salisbury Plain, it was at this time that I had, gained a few new Sergeants in the Company, one sticks to mind Paul, in his younger days I would suspect he was the school bully being a basic coward. I had reason to discipline him this one day, I had just left the mess with one or two under my belt, walking to my room, as I opened the door, all I saw was stars, the little arsehole had whacked me right on the nose, there was blood and snot everywhere. One new Sergeant in arrest and court Marshalled, what a prick. This was how the Regiment was starting to go, frankly they could stuff it, and the type of men we were getting was fucking scum. No character or back bone, gutless wonders. It would be unfair to say that all were no good but it was the beginning of the end. After Battalion training it was time to get ready for the Queens Birthday Parade, "Trooping The Colour" I am not going to harp on this, except to say it was hard work. One day I was the duty Drill Sergeant, after supervising the Royal Guard Change, it was my duty to take the colour off parade. Well I fucked that up as well, I took the wrong Lance Corporals, good job they responded or I would have looked a right prick prancing round Wellington Barracks with no escort to the colour. This red tunic shit was never one of my strong points. I remember one day walking to the Battalion Headquarters, and saw a face from the past, this guy had been a Sergeant, he went absent and ended up in Rhodesia fighting in the army there. When he returned, his only defence at his court marshal was: "how can you expect me to lead men to fight and kill, if I do not even know what it's like?" I am sure he saw plenty in Africa. He was bust down one rank. Six months later he was at the school of infantry as an instructor as a colour Sergeant. Well done, Paul you did it your way. The Battalion was soon to be posted to Germany, Munster, Oxford Barracks. But prior to going the lads had to go and get trained so we were really stretched to the limit for manpower to find the right numbers for all the Royal Guards and duties. The officer corps at this time was just not aware of the pressures placed on the guys, or they just didn't give a shit. I suggested to the Adjutant that I could always pull Guardsman from my arse to help with the manning level, he was not amused. There was no sense of humour in this breed of animal. The Commanding Officer had a regular inspection of the Barracks, and his entourage would follow on. In the Signals stores the concrete floor had a big hole in it. The Boss and entourage were all looking down at the hole, I was asked what was being done about the hole in the ground? I said, quick as a flash.

"IT'S BEING LOOKED INTO", "SIR". I said

STEVE RUDGE

The RSM got the joke, but it flew over the others heads. No sense of humour.

Calvary Barracks Hounslow was always a dump. Patricia and I had a married quarter in Windsor, and for a while the moaning stopped. It was nice, and it was good that Adam and Emma (my kids) could come to visit. They did think it very strange that Sunday lunch consisted of Burger chips and popcorn; what ever happened to roast beef and Yorkshire puddings?

I was driving around in a black XR3. It was a total nightmare driving with Patricia as she was used to zipping along the roads at 55MPH top whack, so there was me cruising along at 70MPH! All she would do is bitch, moan and tell me to slow down. I did moderate my speed for a while but seemed to never get any where fast. It was like driving Miss Daisy! It got to the point that I was getting my self worked up, so enough was enough, this day on a trip up to Grantham to see the kids, she's moaning about my speed, I flipped my lid and said if you don't like it get the fuck out of the car and walk, and went up and down the road to Grantham like Nigel Mansell. Funny, the bitching stopped. Well for a while at least.

The Battalion was still in the throws of its preparations to move to Germany. My boss had worked a flanker, and was away for all the work. The vast majority being done by myself. I was required to get the Company packed up ready to move with the families and all their kit; I was responsible for 180 men and getting them and all their kit to Munster in Germany. Needless to say I was kept really busy, but I still found time to visit the Sergeant's Mess for happy hour on a Friday. The bloody drink drive rules curtailed ones drinking. The camaraderie, however, was always good, and like a breath of fresh air after a hard week's work.

Before the time that Patricia I were married, a few of the guys including myself, took a night out on the razz. We ended up at a Disco in

STEVE RUDGE

Richmond on Thames, the music was loud and it was full of the fairer sex.

I asked John if he had brought us to a ladies gay bar!

"Not so" "it's grab a granny night, Richmond style!" says John.

I had to admit that there was a better class of female than Folkestone. A few pints down my neck and I was getting into the mood for a trip around the floor. Looking around the room there were a couple of girls, one was an old hag the other was really cute. Why is it that there is always one that's a dog? This pair had it down to fine art. Guys would ask to dance with them, and just as the music was to end they would say thank you and walk off the floor only having the one dance with the guy.

John bet me to ask the cute one to dance.

"Yeah" says me.

"I've got three hopes, Bob Hope, no hope and fucking envelope!

A GUARDSMAN'S LOT

"No, go on. I'll dance with the grotty one." says John.

Good old John, he never did have any morals. So off we ventured the whole operation having been discussed as if going into battle. With our plan of action set, off we went. I asked the cute one if she would like to dance.

"Yes, that would be nice", she responded.

John Travolta in blue blazer and slacks zipping round the dance floor. Plan A was in action, as the music was just about to end,

"Thank you" I said

And walked off the floor without looking back. John did the same. It must have shaken the two of them as we did to them what they normally do to others, a bit of reverse psychology! We moved around, dancing with that one and this one, until I saw that the cute one was giving me the look. I wandered over to her and asked if I could buy her a drink?

"Yes please," "vodka and coke." she says.

I was shocked; I really had expected to get the big fuck off.

So there I am with the best looking girl in the house and getting on like a house on fire! Pam was her name, a professional Latin American dance teacher, a one time winner of the all England championships. At five foot one she was all set in the right places, we became an item on and off.

I used to drive her around the UK when I was not working so that she could judge competitions. She was always abroad, always teaching or judging. It was fun if I was with her, but my work had to be done as well, so we really did not have too much time together. It was not long until we split up and that was that, or so I thought.

Moving on

A GUARDSMAN'S LOT

The move to Oxford barracks in Munster Germany was an uneventful one, everyone that should be there got there safe and sound.

It was strange for me, the last time I was in Munster I was married to Susan, then as a fresh young Guardsman living in a shit flat. But this time I was a Warrant Officer married to Patricia, and was given a big fuck off house just around the corner from the Barracks. And just for once Patricia was quite impressed and stopped moaning, so at least something was right in the world for now.

I was still the Company Sergeant Major of Support Company and found myself with a new Company Commander. He seemed OK, but I really didn't have much time to get to know him.

No sooner had I got to Germany and started to settle down then my life started to turn to shit.

Being on the loan service list, which meant I could be sent any where around the world to other armies for training or whatever Her Majesty's Government would have me do.

I received a call from the Ministry of Defence asking if I would like to take up a posting to Lesotho as the Training Officer at the rank of local Captain.

"Yes please" say I,

"No problems", they say.

Two weeks later I received via the Battalion my posting order, to move to Lesotho at the rank of local Captain. Well, well, well. I have been knocking the Officer Corps for years, and now they want to make me a plastic one, no probs I can live with that.

But, other black forces were at work, and certain people had other ideas for the life and times of Steve Rudge. Here am I, thinking all the years that I have given the regiment and all the crap I have done for them, which will at the end of the day cost me two marriages and two children.

A GUARDSMAN'S LOT

The shame of those in power.

With my posting to Lesotho imminent I had made arrangements to talk to the guy that I was to take over from. We settled on the agreement that I would buy his horses and most of his furniture, and that I would import a Land Rover. So we sold all our shit and car, and even got as far as packing our boxes ready to ship over there to Africa.

Patricia and I were really on a high, complaints stopped dead. I had even arranged with a young Captain, who was soon to leave the service, to buy his uniforms. We were all set to go within six weeks.

"Company Sergeant Major" the RSM said,

"Sir" I say,

"The Commanding Officer would like to see you on orders today" he says.

"Why, Sir?" I say,

"Ordered to attend" he says.

STEVE RUDGE

There I am, thinking that he wants to see me to wish me luck and congratulate me! "Well", what the fucking hell did I know?

I marched in and was told that the regiment had decided that Rudge was not going and that I should think again. To say that I was dumbfounded was an understatement. When the shock of what had been said to me had sunk in,

"WHY?" I asked

At this point the Commanding officer was starting to ramble on about crap. I saw through his shit, and requested to see the Regimental Lieutenant Colonel, who is senior to the commanding officer. Bearing in mind that I used to be the Regimental Lieutenants Colonels driver, and therefore I would have expected a fair hearing from him. He was due to visit the Battalion the following Friday.

I went home that night feeling very angry and upset. I could not believe that the finest regiment in the British Army could treat any

A GUARDSMAN'S LOT

one in such a disgraceful manner. The Rudge household that night was not a happy one, even the bitching started again. I couldn't really blame her.

While waiting for Friday to come round I did a bit of investigating. It transpired that the young man that I was going to buy his uniform from had inadvertently mentioned that he was going to sell me his uniforms. However, one of the little stuck-up public school boys arse fuckers had made a comment to the effect of

"Why should Rudge wear the uniform of a Grenadier Captain, when I went to Sandhurst to get my Commission?"

It was as I had thought, nothing other than pure snobbery and class distinction. That was why the commanding officer was babbling on; he could not come out and say:

"Yes you're the man for the job, but not in our uniform."

It was just not politically correct, and he could find himself in big shit from the politicians and the media. Knowing the truth made me even angrier. Friday comes, and I am marched in and get told that it's confirmed and that I will not be going to Lesotho. I asked five times "WHY?" He was unwilling to answer; I even suggested that if it was a uniform issue (so he knew that I knew) that I would use coke bottle tops as pips! He said.

"That's not the point."

I then asked him to explain what the point was? This again was not answered. I explained to him that if he was unable to answer my question then I would have no other alterative than to submit a Redress of Grievance.

Now this would be really heavy shit. The reasons for this are that the Redress must go up the chain of command until answered, eventually, ending up on the Prime Minister's desk. At this time it was good old Maggie Thatcher, and as she was looking for votes from the working class, I believe that She would

A GUARDSMAN'S LOT

never have allowed this type of behaviour from her Officers.

"Knowing this", these gutless wonders could never now admit that I knew the real reason for me not going to Lesotho. Snobbery, nothing more and nothing less. I was more than qualified, approved by a higher authority and the posting order issued not only to me but to the Battalion. So they knew what and why but failed to do anything until some little gobshite spoke. So let the Games begin.

I typed up the Redress and submitted it to my boss. Of course he could not answer it, and passed it on to the commanding officer. No sooner had he received it, I got a call from my boss and I was sent home. I had my command taken off me. In other words, I was sacked but on full pay. The term is called gardening leave, stay at home until further notice. Enjoy you say? No it's bloody awful. I was highly motivated and not one to lie around twiddling my thumbs. I had been lied to by what we thought were officers and gentlemen. The worst crooks in the world are the upper crust of society· they don't give a shit who gets hurt. One of the main hurtful things was, that I was also ostracised by my fellow peers, for the first time in my Army service I felt totally alone. Patricia was as much use as a chocolate tea pot, moaning and bitching even more now. I really could not blame her, as she really didn't understand the seriousness of what was going on.

The Regiment was playing the stalling game I was called into the Battalion once or twice a week to be marched in like some two week old recruit, asked the same question:

"Had I changed my mind? "I would be asked.

My response was the same,

"No, please answer the redress and tell me why?"

Their answers were never relevant to the question asked, so I would be sent off home again, it was becoming very frustrating.

A GUARDSMAN'S LOT

But I refused let them drag me down; they knew they were in the wrong; otherwise the Redress would have gone through as fast as a speeding bullet.

Eventually after two months I was summoned to the Brigade Headquarters to be interviewed by the Brigade Commander, The Brigadier (now an arm chair General on some television network, saying how he would win the wars he's not involved in). I was marched in again, so much for interview techniques, I was made to feel like a crook. He asked me:

"What do you expect me to do about this?"

My answer was crisp and to the point,

"Sir, please answer the question, why? Or pass it on to a higher authority to someone who can."

I was told that I was really being quite childish. Their only defence of their operant and dishonourable conduct was to try and knock me down and belittle me, well I was having none of it. I said to him:

STEVE RUDGE

"With all due respect sir, which is something you are failing to show me, please answer the Redress or move it on to someone who can."

"I cannot answer the question", he said

I saluted and thanked him for wasting my time and walked out of his office. I didn't even wait for the Garrison RSM to march me out, whom came bounding after me. I stopped in my tracks, turned on my heels and just glared at him. He got the message in point fuck of a second, and disappeared back into the Brigadier's office. I walked out, caught the bus and went home, again, to await the next round. I think the message was getting to them: this guy is not going to budge, and by Christ I was not going to move my stand point.

After a few days at home I was sent for again, this time by the Adjutant; a young captain who's job was to suck up to people senior than himself and keep the junior officers in toe.

A GUARDSMAN'S LOT

This time the tactics were different, he was asking me if I would I be interested in other job?

"Well yes" "so long as it was on the same type of package" I responded.,

The damn job he offered was four months separation from my wife as the liaison officer, at my same rank, in the United States of America near the Rocky Mountains. I asked him if he was out of his tree, how was this similar to two years in Africa?

"But yes" "you could have it if you withdrew your redress" he said.

Was this clown fucking mad and did he really think I was a total prick? I didn't even bother to answer him. I walked out of his office and went home.

Apparently he was given a bollocking from his boss as he didn't have any authority to offer me a lollypop let alone try and negotiated with me. So now this little gobshite was yet another enemy of mine. Surprise, surprise I was summoned again to see the Adjutant, this time he was in a fighting mood, suits me fine I thought. The conversation was really all one sided, his. He was trying to tell me how silly I was to pursue this matter, and that I really should review my position. After he had mentioned my position about five times, I had heard enough of this public school boy telling me, a father of two with more experience in my dick than he would ever have, about my position. So I told him my position:

"I have been fucked about by you people for over two months;" "you tried to blackmail me into withdrawing my complaint. I have sold all my possessions and my car. I walk or take the bus like a god damn gypsy, and to top it all my family are suffering as a result of all this!" I said, getting angry.

His response to my outburst was:

"I really don't give a damn about you or your family."

That was as far as he got, I really lost it. The next thing I do remember is the RSM dragging me off this little fool. And me storming out of the office.

"How fucking dare you!" I said

The RSM was shouting after me to.

"Stand still".

I retorted by saying:

"You better just fuck off or you will get some as well."

Yes you got it, I then went home. After I had cooled off, I had visions I would be arrested and court martialled or worse, be thrown out! Patricia was calling me a fucking fool; For once I had to agree with her. I thought I was well and truly fucked. I saw no one nor heard anything from anyone for days. They must have reasoned that young prissy little officers and gentlemen must not tell a senior warrant officer that he doesn't care about the guy's family. Even if you don't give a flying fuck for him or his family you don't ever say so, he should have known better. I bet he does today the wanker. I kept myself sane during this stressful time by running. I would don my running kit and just run for about two hours, pounding the roads of Munster to cool off- to keep my head straight, getting ready for the next round.

There is a funny twist to all those months of anguish and it all would have been for nothing, and I was going to get my Waterloo. When the axe fell, it would be from a totally unexpected source.

Chapter 18.
Judas.

On the day of the long knives, Patricia and I had been arguing. I don't even remember what about. I knew that I now had them on the back foot and soon they would have to move it on to the next level which would be the Ministry of Defence. These were the guys who said originally that I could go, so we were so close to the final round.

I needed to get the fuck away from Patricia and her mouth so I donned my running kit and disappeared for a couple of hours. While running I was thinking that really I had been a bit of a shit and that after my run I would buy a bottle of wine and a good video and make my peace with Patricia. So when I arrived near to my house I took a detour and went to the bank to cash a cheque for one hundred Marks. Frau Kunt, the manger, tells me that I am overdrawn. Not possible, all the money for Africa was in the account. I thought that it must be another guy called Rudge. Easy mistake to make. So I called in to the shops and collected the wine and video, then went home and put the wine in the fridge.

Patricia was not in but I didn't think much of it, she must have gone shopping. So I got showered and changed, jumped on the bus and went down town. I knew where she liked to visit, but could not find her. She must be at home by now. So I took the bus back home, still no sign of her. After about an hour, I was getting a bit worried, something was not right. I went and looked in the wardrobe. Yeah, you guessed it, clothes missing, passport gone, and

A GUARDSMAN'S LOT

guess what? Frau Kunt was right; the fucking bitch had done a runner with all the cash. So on top of all the Army crap I was left penniless and really alone, nice one Patricia! The knife was well and truly stuck in, and twisted for good measure, then ripped out. I was really in a state of despair. How dare she! I would not have minded. All she had to do was ask and I really would have let her go. So now that she had made her bed she must lie in it, So I found all her possessions that she had left and gave the lot away to charity. The German Red Cross were at least happy. In total I gave away three large box loads of her crap!

Now word had got out that she had left, the RSM came round to see if I was OK, Well that's what he said. He was even trying to be pleasant. His parting words made me sit up and take notice:

"Steve," he said, "you realise that the job you were hoping to get, well one of the criteria is that you must have your family with you. It's not for a single person."

Was I fucked or what? She had managed to achieve in two hours what the Regiment couldn't do in nearly four months, so the posting was cancelled and the Redress thrown out. There must have been great delight in the Officer's mess. Now you understand why I think their a bunch of gutless clueless cunts.

I was granted two weeks leave and was getting posted to the Guard's Depot again, this time as the training Warrant Officer. Big Deal. Just like Africa, eh? I had no money to buy a stamp let alone an air ticket to UK. Thanks to my Mum and Dad, they sent funds over to me and I got the fuck away from the Battalion and went home to Stockton on Tees feeling let down and totally deflated.

While at my parent's house I received a phone call from my Regimental headquarters in London, they wanted to see me. So I went down there to see what they wanted. I did have

A GUARDSMAN'S LOT

another reason to go though to London, as I had been talking to Pam and had arranged to visit her on the day I went down to London. While at Regimental Headquarters I was told that my holiday in August was not to be and that I was to go to Porteuos camp in Sherwood Forest and teach the Army Cadet staff on how to be instructors. I left Regimental Headquarters and made my way to see Pam. She was working till late and I had to hang around until about ten o'clock that night near to Richmond. When we met it was all very strange. I told her my sad fucked up life to date over dinner. She must have felt sorry for me. The rest of the night was a great moral booster, I don't know if she had changed or I had but then we were back on the merry go round, again. I really have to say that my ego had taken a pounding and she really did help me through a real bad time in my life. I used to run her around England to her dancing venues weekends in Blackpool. We both enjoyed the same things and for a while it was great, so, for the good times, Pam, I really thank you.

I needed a car and borrowed a few pounds off my Dad, so en-route to Porteuos camp in my great big silver Rover I wondered what the Regiment had dicked me for now? Well they may have thought that I was being dicked. Let me tell you, I met some great guys and had a ball over that four week period. I was in my element teaching them all my skills and how they should also teach drill, weapons, tactics and map reading. But most importantly how to have a good time, at work and a better time in the mess. It was just what I needed to get me back on track and get my head straight. I could not write this without a mention to Andy Axten, we met when he was one of my students. He was one of the brighter stars; we were and still are the best of friends. Andy is a Captain in the cadets and good luck to him. He could teach a few of the Regiment's officers how to treat people. "Well done Andy". The Rover served me

A GUARDSMAN'S LOT

well on this training, carrying me up and down to London at weekends. The fuel bills were a bit steep, but the army were paying the travel bills so that was fine, and the car was fast and comfortable.

The time came and I had to say a fond farewell to all my new mates at Porteuos and head towards Pirbright in Surrey, back to the Guards Depot. I moved into a little room in the Sergeant's mess and unpacked all my kit getting it sorted out, ready for me to start work the next day. The job was a real bitch; I had to write all the training programmes for the whole of the Guard's depot. It was a hell of a task, at times. When I first started, I was still working 'till gone ten at night. I soon got on top of it and by Wednesday of each week the time was pretty much my own. One of my fellow training team members was a guy called Patrick. . He too had been shafted by the Army, so we had an instant connection. We were good mates for a long time

STEVE RUDGE

until he also shafted me. That story will come later.

Word must have been sent that Rudge was a trouble maker, so I was given a hard time from the RSM and others who like to bully people. It was water off a duck's back to me. I just did my job, made no major fuck ups and kept out of their way. I visited Pam when ever I could, which was always interesting to say the least.

Patricia, had managed to track me down from the States and was calling me on the phone a couple of times a week. She was trying to make me feel sorry for her sounding all down in the dumps. I was also formulating a plan for her. So I started to encourage her a little. After a while the question was put to me

"Steve do you think we can try again?" she says.

"Well"! "Yes" I said.

And that was that, Patricia was coming back. I set the wheels in motion to get a married quarter and fit it out for her.

A GUARDSMAN'S LOT

I met her at Heathrow and drove her home, no bitching about the car's speed, well things were improving. She arrived on the Thursday night, after my work on Friday I went to the mess had a couple of pints and went home got changed and went to see Pam for the weekend. I arrived home at six AM on the Monday morning, and Patricia was beside herself with worry.

"Where have you been? She says

It's not fair that you just disappear for two days and leave no word. I have called every where for you!" she said.

"Not every where" I said with a little grin,

She was now demanding to know where I had been. I was really cool and said nothing, I got ready for work and just before I left the house I delivered the final blow. I handed her a one way ticket to Atlanta USA and a suitcase and said.

"Your flight leaves at eight o'clock tonight". I said.

"You know how to get to airports by yourself" "as you're well practiced". "Now you leave on my terms", "and please remember this lesson, do not ever do to a man what you did to me ever again". I continued.

"Goodbye." I said finally.

Then I left for the office; tell you what I felt good, revenge as a food is always better, when delivered cold. When I got back that night she had left.

I only ever heard from her one time after our divorce, it must have been two years after that event, she phoned me from the States in a right state crying and sobbing, she tells me that she had met a guy called Doug and that they had married and that three months into this wonderful marriage the other three wives popped out of the woodwork. My, my, Doug had been a busy boy and was a bigamist four times over. I gave her my words of wisdom:

"IT COULDN'T HAPPEN TO A NICER PERSON. BYE, BYE, PATSY."

Chapter 19.
The Stockbroker Period.

While at Pirbright, the Thatcher Government was selling off all its assets. I found that by buying these shares at the time of issue and selling them as soon as I got them I could make thirty percent profit. So I moved into the stock market stage of my life. The economy was flying, and I managed to make a few bucks over a period of time. Patrick was also on the same kick. For whatever reason I sold my shares a week before black Monday (that's when the bubble burst). Patrick lost thirty thousand pounds in twenty four hours.

STEVE RUDGE

I was in the end of service mode. I had just over two years to do and my promotion prospects were minus zero. So I used my time, and the army time for me and fuck the Regiment.

I was sending my CV out to all and sundry, and all major Companies in and around London. There am I thinking, that as this exercise is part of my leaving the army soon, so fuck it, I will let them pay the postage. Big, big mistake.

While wheeling and dealing my CV through the postal system, it back fired on me. Thank fuck that the bosses had all changed over by then.

I sent one of my CVs to the Ford Motor Company- another mistake.

I was taking in the ambience of my office one morning when the door flies open and in walks this Military Police Corporal-

"Are you Sergeant Major Rudge.?" He says

"Get the fuck out of my office. Knock on the fucking door. Wait till I say come in and then put your fucking feet together if you wish to

A GUARDSMAN'S LOT

speak to me and then you can call me Sir. Now get the fuck out and try again." I screamed at him.

I was in my bad mood mode, and apart from which, I fucking hate Military policemen.

In he comes feet and arms flying around as if he is on drugs, banging around shouting.

"Sir!" he screams.

"Come in young man take a seat, can I get you some coffee?" I said, as nice as pie.

That took the wind out off his sails and put him right off his guard.

After a long chat I discovered that the security manager at Ford was an ex military policeman. The bastard had sent my CV to the army police, to fuck me up after he had spotted the army postage mark, what an arsehole!

So I was to be investigated for misuse of army property. The young corporal left my office with the facts as I gave to him. Which were: I am soon to leave the army and was seeing how the land lies in civvy street when job hunting. I don't think I would get a job at Ford somehow anymore. The RMP said he would pass on my interview notes to his boss and that I would have to await the outcome of the investigation. I would then be notified. He did ask me one question which was:

"Is this the only one I had sent via the army system?" He asked.

"Yes, "of course it was." I said

Yeah right.

These things take time and the months moved on.

The boss of my department was a guy called Neil, he was also a Grenadier. Of a higher rank but lower on brains. He was the standard yes man, and a complete arse. He made life difficult for Patrick and I, as he had no one else to boss around, not that we took much notice of him any way. But he could make my life worse because he was well liked in the regiment. He had a nasty bully boy attitude in him, and he also took an unhealthy interest in other people's business.

A GUARDSMAN'S LOT

Neil would always be short of money, and would supplement his wages by selling army kit to junior ranks. I had overheard a conversation between Neil and one of the sergeants, to arrange for a meeting so that Neil could sell this poor guy some kit. Money dealings between ranks is a big no, no in the army, so I saved this information in my memory banks, one never knows when one might need it. As it happens one of the lads in Germany had swapped his car for my XR3 as mine was tax paid and his was not. I got permission from my boss to do the deal and it was done. He saved £2000.00 on taxes and I had a nice new car. He took up his posting in London happy as a sand boy with his XR3 and I sold his car as part of my posting to Lesotho.

Eighteen months after I had traded cars with this little shit, in comes Neil shouting that Regimental Headquarters in London (that's where this clown had been posted) wanted me to pay this little prick £2000.00 because the

XR3 had been in an accident apparently when I owned it. "Don't think so" says I. The saga would not go away and all the time Neil was stirring the pot and taking what Regimental Headquarters said as gospel, so fuck me. I went to a lawyer in Aldershot who explained in twenty seconds, that to even worry about it was nonsense, as I was not a dealer and bills of transfer were signed there was no case and if he wanted to go to court, bring it on. Back at the office the next day, in comes Neil shouting his mouth off telling me to pay the guy or he will have to take disciplinary action against me. I had really had a shit load of this crap from him. I jumped to my feet shut the door and put my face into his

"Listen you," I said

"I am fed up with you nosing into my business and my private affairs. The car has got fuck all to do with you and further more if you start your shit with me again I will walk over to the Commandant's office and mention to him that you have been selling Army kit to junior ranks." I said

He tried to shout over me and bluff it, threatening to have me arrested. I did no more than put my cap on and left my office, my intentions him must have been obvious.

"Steve, Steve, Steve. Wait a moment". He whines.

"Now you come to mention it I will phone Regimental Headquarters and tell them that they really should not get involved, as it is a civil matter." He continues.

I said nothing and walked out of the exit. I didn't go to the Commandant and really I don't think I would have anyway, but I let the little fucker sweat. I went into the stores and had a coffee with my mate the Storeman. I let him suffer for a couple of hours then went back to my office. Neil was hovering around my office.

"Is there any I thing I do for you Sir?" I said

"No Steve, are you OK?" He asks.

"Yes I am fine", I say

Then I told him not to worry his little secret was safe.

There after he was as nice as pie, no more shouting or gobbing off and never asked a personal question again. Lesson taught "information is power". The man was short on brains and his greed nearly fucked him. What a plank. As I said, the hierarchy at the Depot had all changed and the new bosses were great. Although in the eyes of the regiment I was lower than snake shit, not that I really gave a damn. The new Commandant used to pop over to my office to have a coffee and discuss the training programmes with me. To make changes for him, he understood the complex issues involved, and really appreciated the fact that I would move heaven and earth to help him. It would cost me time and effort but it was worth it to keep him sweet. No one ever bothered me again at the Depot, and life was sweet; visit Pam, have a beer, play squash, no problems.

A GUARDSMAN'S LOT

My last November at the Guards Depot and it was rugby time. Some tall, skinny streak of piss of a Grenadier Officer, who commanded the boys Company, asked if I would play rugby for the Company. It was to be Grenadiers versus the Welsh Guards.

"Why not?" I said.

I do enjoy rugby, but that twat was not going to find out. I made it sound like I was doing him the favour. I was thirty eight years old, still very fit but not so quick on my feet. The whistle blew, from then till the whistle blew for the end I was thumped kicked and saw more mud than ball. Every cloud has a sliver lining, and mine was in the form of the great long streak of piss, who was stood on the sidelines egging on the boys. As I ran past him I heard "having fun Company Sergeant Major?" with a note of sarcasm in his voice and a smirk on his face. But fate was with me that November afternoon. Lineout, Grenadiers throws in, and not 10 feet away was Mr Streak of piss on the sideline. The ball drops into my hands I pass as hard as I can to my right winger. Fuck me, it's a lousy throw but is travelling through the air like a rocket. Streak of piss gets it full in the face. Both teams stopped in their tracks and went OOOOHH!!!! It was a lousy pass from the scum half, and we lost the lineout, but Mr Smug streak of piss was last seen wondering off the playing field trying to stem a very severe nose bleed. Bless him. He never took the piss again out of me, that's for sure. The game over Welsh Guards won, I didn't really care. I staggered back to the mess and was really very pleased with myself. Hot bath and down to the bar for a few. I walked into the bar and was rewarded by a pint pushed in my hand by the RSM and a big cheer from the gang. Apparently the skinny Major was not that popular, and it was good to be the toast of the mess.

Just as things at Pirbright were getting really good, it was time for me to move on to my final posting before I left the Army. I was

A GUARDSMAN'S LOT

due to go to Princess Marina College, the home of the REME, the Royal Electrical Mechanical Engineers. Arborfeild.

Pirbright would not let me go, as there was some unfinished business to deal with; the matter of the stolen stamp had to be resolved. Sounds like a case for Sherlock Holmes or the start of a new book. Before I go on to explain what happened to me about the missing stamp there is a story that has to be told to explain the outcome of the stamp.

The chief clerk of the guards depot was Dave, also a Warrant officer first class, and consequently senior to me. He was one of my best allies and I never knew the reasons why, he was always very helpful to me and supported me when I was down. One day while I was waiting for the RMP report, I was sat in the mess having a beer, and Dave comes up and starts to talk to me.

"Steve" he says,

"You really don't remember me do you?"

"Well" I said "not really Dave you're the chief clerk."

"No" he says, "before?"

"Well no Dave to be truthful no."

So he starts his story: Well, in 1966 I was in the barrack room next to yours. We had a room inspection and my boots were thrown down the road and stamped on because they were not good enough. I was told that if they were not sorted out by lights out then I would be in real big trouble (Dave never swore). "That was when you saw me nearly in tears outside, and you asked what the problem was?" So I told you, (I still could not remember any of this) and you took the boots off me and in half an hour you had them shinning like black diamonds. The Sergeant passed them and I was not in trouble. I have never forgot that favour from you (I looked at Dave and I swear there were tears in his eyes as he remembered my kindness). Funny how the circle of life moves round. All that time ago, twenty two and a half years down the road and

A GUARDSMAN'S LOT

Dave is going to help me. So the day that the report came back Dave came to my office and told me on the QT, that the RMPs wanted me to be charged with misuse of Military property. I could have been sacked, thrown out, court marshalled or hung at dawn.

Dave had put his knob on a block and convinced the boss that it was such a petty matter and that he should call me in give me a slap on the wrist and let me go to Arborfeild without a blemish.

On my final day, before I was due to leave the Depot, I was summoned to the main office, Dave marched me in to the Commandant, whispering to me not to worry. The commandant said to me

"You know why you're here?"

I said "yes, Sir"

"Then do not do it again and enjoy your new posting to Arborfeild and thank you for all the work you have done for me. Seen, march out." Says the Commandant, smiling.

Out I went thanking who ever made me do that favour twenty two and a half years ago; there must be a God of favourers returned., my last day prior to going on leave, I spent at the mess. They dined me out in true Guards Depot Style, complete with engraved tankard and lashings of Guardsman Blood (port). After a very late night and a long sleep I said my farewells and left Pirbright for a two week holiday with Pam in Greece. Lovely eh?

Chapter 20.
Life Takes a Good Turn.

On my return from Greece I rented a small house in Twickenham. Pam and I were not really hitting it off too well, so separate houses were my idea. It suited me fine. To travel to Arborfeild, which is near Reading, if I didn't feel like driving home I would sleep over in the Mess, which was no big deal. I used to visit Patrick and his girlfriend in north London, go to Discos with Pam when we were together, but our whole relationship was falling apart. It was time for Patrick to retire and he married his girlfriend and moved to Los Angeles. I had a buddy in the Air movement's office in London so I could get to Washington for twelve pounds. It was a gamble to get back as there was only one flight a week, but all the times I visited Patrick in LA I never had a problem, and all curtsey of the Royal Air Force. So I would visit Patrick two or three times a year.

At Arborfeild I was then the Company Sergeant Major of B Company the junior leader's regiment. I was in my element I had totally switch off and was in "wind down" mode, I really didn't give a shit, but what was really amazing was that B Company won all the cups best at drill, highest standards on room inspections the lads must have been shit scared of me, as they really didn't now what to make of me.

The Company Commander was called Trevor, who was a Major from the Medical Corps, the lads nicknamed him "dope on a rope". Not fair really, as he was very good at paper work and reports, but not at being a real soldier. Myself, and Len, "the Company second in command" who was from the Gloucester Regiment, took on that role and let him do the pen pushing. We handled Trevor fine between us. I remember the first day that Len arrived in the Company, having been an ex RSM in his Battalion but was now a Captain. He came to my office and started to try on the old RSM attitude with me, thinking I was some dumb lance corporal, by talking down to me. I was not Going to have two years of this so I got up went to his office and asked if I could talk to him off the record and in private?

"Yes, of course Sergeant Major" he says.

I closed the door.

"Sir, I am the Sergeant Major in this Company. I do the shouting, the rude comments and the barking of orders. You lost that privilege when you got commissioned. So please do not talk to me like that again. I suspect that when you were a Sergeant Major you would not tolerate being spoken to in any other way, other than with respect, so please cut it out, we have to work as a team". I continued.

Thank you, Sir" I said.

And I left his office. At about four o'clock that afternoon Len comes to my office and asked if we had a happy hour on a Friday at the mess? "Yes" Sir "We do."

"Then pack up your office and please invite me to the mess for a pint". Len says.

There after it was Len and Steve and we got on like a house on fire for a long time. No worries.

One of the young guys called Brandon had just arrived in my Company having just completed his induction training with the Recruit Company. He was convinced that he was not cut out to be an army man. One of my roles as Company Sergeant Major was the troop's welfare. Brandon arrived at my office and was telling me that he wanted to go home. My tactics, that I used to employ was to try and postpone the young men from making the wrong decisions. I would try and talk them into staying for at least one more week. Most of the problems were that these young men were homesick. Everyone who joined went through being homesick and the best cure is time, Brandon agreed to give it another week. I must admit that I saw something in this young man, there was something about him. He was bright, he only had to stay a year with B Company and then he would move to man's service and his trade training would really kick off. I managed to keep Brandon in the REME and within eight weeks he was promoted, with a little help from myself of course.

What I had seen in him came out, he was a born leader. I told him that if he were to keep up with what he was doing I would think he would make Junior RSM before he left.

In his final three months, Brandon having moved through the ranks to be my junior Company Sergeant Major was promoted to junior RSM. I was really pleased for him. So now he was to be trained in more military matters. For a start, at the end of each term there was a big passing out parade. The boys are trained by the Company Sergeant Majors and practiced, but the final parade is taken by the Boys. So Brandon had his work cut out for himself. I helped him and spent a lot of my own time making sure that he knew the parade inside out, there is nothing more embarrassing than standing out there in front of hundreds of people and then freezing in mid-flow. I really should not have worried, Brandon, performed like a trooper. The parade went really well, and afterwards he and his family are invited into the Mess for lunch and drinks. It was here that Brandon and family were told by the Commandant that Brandon had been recommended for a Commission within the REME. The officer Corps in the REME is nothing like the Gobshites of the Grenadiers. Brandon wandered over to me and said:

A GUARDSMAN'S LOT

"Sir, thank you for all that you have done for me,

And thank you for making me stay in when I wanted to leave." Says Brandon.

That was nice of him I thought, and then Len and I went to the bar and had a couple of drinks.

After the passing out parade, the place would close down and most of the boys and staff would go on leave. The life for the staff at Arborfeild was really very laid back. In the summer we would have cricket with a Pimms bar, complimented by strawberries, all very civilised. The training exercises were not much worse, it was always near a pub! We would all have tents, no roughing it for anybody; even the boys enjoyed it, like a Boy Scout camp! We used to teach them basic skills but in a very informal manner. These kids were bright and did not need too much supervision. It really was a joy. Len and I would worry about the training and

STEVE RUDGE

Trevor would worry about Len and me. We used to have a real good laugh.

On one of my trips into London I met a girl called Tammy; she was from Boston (USA). We went out for a while. She worked in London, near Queensway, with a nice flat on the edge of Nottinghill. In fact she was a bit of a nutcase-driving round London on her Harley Davidson. She had a well paid job, and on one of my leaves from Arborfeild we went to visit Patrick in LA. She hired a five litre ford mustang soft top, what a dream! We went shopping on Rodeo Drive and we took in all that LA had to offer. Tammy would not let me spend a penny; I was starting to feel like a pimp! She bought for me a lovely camel hair coat, a wonderful deer skin jacket, American express that will do nicely madam! After LA we flew to Boston to visit her Mum. The house that she called home was set in the old part of town, four stories high! Going to bed was a marathon on its own. She should have had a lift installed. I really must admit the house

A GUARDSMAN'S LOT

was quite impressive, it was Boston old Money. We had nights out and saw her old buddies; it really was a nice time. I was impressed with Boston a nice city. We met Tammy's daughter whom had just finished university at Harvard, a very bright kid. Tammy was starting to get a bit to serious in our relationship after we had returned from the States. It was time to cool down a bit and take stock of my life. I really wasn't ready for any thing serious in my life yet. I was having too much fun. So Tammy and I parted, or so I thought.

One of my favourite things to do if I had a weekend off was to drive up to Halifax in Yorkshire on a Friday night. Getting out of London was a fucking nightmare! On one trip it must have taken me three hours just to get to the M1, and then the traffic didn't thin out until we were nearly there. Good job the clubs didn't liven up till late. Halifax was renowned for its night life. I will not go into too much detail, but a good night was always on the cards. Friday and Saturday nights the town used to bounce.

I was given the grand job of being the Sergeants Mess Treasurer for six months. I had a lady that did all the book work, so really I had even less to do. I used to wander round the mess looking for work. On one of my many boring trips I came across a young woman standing in the reception area. What drew my attention to her was what she was wearing, the main features being pink socks and white trainers. I, being polite, asked if I could help her?. Very cheekily she replied:

"No thanks". She said

I thought at first "Cheeky cow", it wasn't until sometime later that I discovered that she was, in fact, one of the Mess employees. So much for me being on the ball! Things at work continued in the same boring vein for the next week or so, me looking for work to do and finding nothing. Other than, as Treasurer, one of my duties was to empty and refill the slot machine in the bar.

A GUARDSMAN'S LOT

As this is cash, a fellow Mess member always had to be present, just in case I was so bored that I took the money and fucked off to Blackpool. This one machine over a period between Friday and Monday could make a Mess profit in excess of £4,000. One of the sergeants, Dickie, had a major gambling problem, as Treasurer it was apparent that I would see who the fools were who would waste their wives housekeeping on a stupid machine. It came to the point, in Dickie's case, that his monthly Mess bill exceeded his wages. I eventually had to ban this young man from playing the machines and ordered the bar staff that "Dickie could have drinks on account but not cash". He came to my office pleading like a junkie, needing his fix to please allow him back on the machines. I had to be really tough with him and said if I ever caught him on the machines he would be banned from the Mess and probably disciplined as well. One particular Friday myself and the President of the Messing Committee, a chap called Colin, emptied the

STEVE RUDGE

machines. We took the cash back to the office for counting along with the meter readings. We sat there for 2 hours trying to balance the books. There was in fact in excess of £100 in cash too much which we could not account for. We waited for the bookkeeper to come back from lunch and asked her to double check her figures. We were still in excess of £100, must have been a temporary fault with the cash in meter. So at 1600 hrs the bar was opened for happy hour. Dickie was in the bar having a pint when Colin and I walked in, Colin was holding a cash bag full of coins which he tipped on the bar and told the barman "The drinks are on the house". Dickie, seeing all the pound coins, went into total withdrawal. When the free pints were finished it was rumoured that he left the Mess in tears. I wouldn't blame him if he did because all the Mess members were telling Dickie maybe the £100 on the bar could have won him the jackpot.

A GUARDSMAN'S LOT

I eventually discovered who the young lady was in pink socks, her name was Jan and frankly I was very attracted to her as she was gorgeous. I used to talk to her whenever I got the chance and eventually asked her if she would like to go for lunch. I was also entering uncharted waters as far as my morals were concerned as she was a married woman. I have never knowingly hit on a married woman before but there was something about Jan which wouldn't go away. After several attempts, Jan's friend Gwen, who also worked in the Mess, but had appalling body odour, convinced Jan that she had nothing to lose as I seemed like a nice guy. Finally Jan agreed to go to lunch with me. Now I had to impress her so I booked a table at the Hilton Hotel just outside Sunningdale, picked Jan up in my car, she was looking lovely and this time...no pink socks. There was only one glitch at lunch, which turned out to be a dirty fork which I promptly sent back for a replacement. Jan must have thought me, as she later admitted, to be a complete arse. A few glasses of wine, a nice meal and we were getting on extremely well. Jan's family come from the North East of England near Newcastle, she was married to a Corporal in the REME called Billy who was a complete bullyboy. At this stage in our relationship I knew that if we pursued what we were pursuing someone or all would get hurt, so I tried to keep things at arms length, I tried to enjoy the moment, but found it increasingly hard to maintain and control my feelings. Jan was like a drug to me I could not let go, so drastic action had to be taken. Billy had found out that we were together, and Jan was getting doubts so I sent her back to Billy and told her to make her marriage work. After about a week I got a phone call from Jan, she was stuck in Newcastle. Billy had taken them to visit her Mum and at sometime over the weekend had jumped in his car and fucked off back to Arborfield. Leaving Jan with the dog and no means of getting home, she asked for

A GUARDSMAN'S LOT

my help. I told her to "wait until midnight at the cash point, then at one second after, draw out the money you need."

"Billy had done that the night before". Jan said to me.

"Then get the train to Reading and I will meet you at the station" "just let me know what time you are due to arrive." I said.

The next day at about seven o'clock in the evening she arrived at Reading. I wanted so much to take her to my place in Twickenham, but no, I was going to be strong, so I took her to her house, and dropped her off outside.

"Any problems please call me". I said.

I went back to the Mess and got hammered. My feelings were all over the place. What a mess I was in. But if it was going to work she had to be 100% certain that her marriage was finished. I would not allow myself to influence any of her decisions. To say I was miserable was only scratching the surface. I was getting paid to work, so I set myself to task and continued my

STEVE RUDGE

Sergeants Mess duties, which meant walking around looking busy or playing squash.

On one of my tours around the Mess I caught a glimpse of someone that looked like Jan. Whoever it was turned away from me and walked around the corridor. I didn't think much about it until Gwen suggested that I go to the staff room and see what's there. I took her advice and made my way to the staff room. What I saw was a shock even for me. Poor Jan was sat there with half her face bruised and the other half unrecognisable and swollen. I told her to get into my car and took her home to Twickenham. Her whole body was covered in bruises and welts. I suggested that I take her to hospital, but she was having none of it. The next best thing I could do was take photographs of all the damage to her poor body. The finger marks around the neck were starting to turn a nasty colour blue/black. I took Jan back to the Mess after she had rested. I spoke to the RSM and got permission for Jan to stay in the Mess

A GUARDSMAN'S LOT

until we could resolve the matter. The RSM was more than accommodating, so I arranged a room for Jan and put her to bed. I kept trying to convince her to charge Billy with assault and to go to the Police. She refused. The next day after a poor nights sleep, Jan was feeling very sore. Her one worry though was that her gold chain, that I had given her, was still in the house with Billy and she did not want the little creep to throw it away. So when I finished work that night, Jan and I jumped in the car and drove round to the house. I knocked on the door. Billy answered wearing a towel around his waist, saw Jan and said:

"What the fuck do you want? You got me out of the bath."

Billy made a gesture and I thought he was going to try and hit me. I had restrained myself long enough, the red mist came down. I thumped Billy in the face and kept hitting him all the way up the stairs. I really did loose it. I was shouting at him:

STEVE RUDGE

"Sorry to disturb your bath" I said

And threw him in the tub. I was holding him under the water. I should have drowned the little cunt of a wife beater, in fact I nearly did. All this time Jan was sitting down stairs. I was in the process of looking for a razor blade to cut his fucking eyes out when I heard Jan shouting for me, saying:

"That's enough!" she says.

It will never be enough for me, and if I see the little shit ever again he will get more of the same.

In hindsight, just as well she did stop me otherwise I would now be doing life for murder. On the way out of the house I surveyed the damage; the walls were covered in blood (not mine). I put Jan in the car and drove back to the Mess. We were both in need of a stiff drink.

The next morning I was in the accounts office after I had delivered the photos for processing, and there was a knock on the door. Outside were a policeman and policewoman.

A GUARDSMAN'S LOT

"Are you Mr Rudge?" I am asked.

"Yes of course, can I help you?" I replied.

The policeman informed me, that "a charge of assault had been made against me, and did I know any thing about it?"

"Of course I know what you're talking about" I said,

I was not going to deny anything. So I told them my story, and how we went back to the house to collect the chain he answered the door and tried to attack me. As a trained soldier I defended myself to the best of my ability. I admitted I may have been a little harsh, but that's the way it goes. Furthermore there was good reason for me losing it.

"What do you mean?" The policewoman said.

"Can you please trust me for twenty minutes and I will show you?" I asked.

I jumped into the car and drove back to the chemist to collect the photographs and returned to the awaiting police officers who were happy to sit and have a coffee. I found Jan with the police and she was giving them her side of the story, bless her she really did look in a mess, the bruises were now worse than ever. I took out the photographs and handed them to the policewoman, her expressions said it all. The police officers asked Jan to lay a charge of assault against Billy, which she did. The policeman said to me that they were coming here to arrest me, but now they had to go and arrest Billy and that I had nothing to answer for. Yet again my guardian angel was looking after me; Billy had been a Corporal in the REME and I as a Warrant Officer. I could have been in big shit for striking a junior rank, but luckily for me the day that Billy got fucked over by me was also the day that Billy got discharged out of the Army. He was not having a good civvy life. Jan dropped the charges Billy against my advice and set in motion the divorce against Billy. She moved in to my house in Twickenham and all was well. I told the RSM about the goings on just to cover my arse; he was fine about it all.

All this time and for the last 2 years I had been heavily into the freemasons and used to attend the lodge at least once a week. Each year the lodge puts on a big dinner night for wives as well as the men. As the Sergeants Mess Treasurer I was in the perfect position to accommodate the lodge. I cleared it with the RSM to use the Mess for the dinner, I even arranged for the college pipe band to play. The pipe Major is also a fellow Mason. The lodge would get a first rate service at really good prices and the mess would get a good deal of profit to boost the Mess funds. We invited the RSM and Sue, his wife. The whole night was a real success, and the Master of the lodge presented me with a gold set of engraved cuff links to say thank you. It was a really nice gesture. The only glitch was, that one of the Mess members got drunk and started to take the piss out of the Masons. He had been in the bar half the day and was really becoming a pain in the arse, as I was the only Mess member at the dinner it really was down to me to try and calm this guy down, I had a word with him but he just got even more loud and aggressive. One of the lodge members who was also a police detective (in fact ninety percent of the lodge were all police in one way or another) overheard this clown telling me that if I didn't fuck off he would smack me in the mouth. The fellow Mason pulled out his warrant card and advised Mr Pisshead that he could be locked up for threatening behaviour. This did the job and the drunk staggered off to bed. The drunk, came to find me in the morning and was so very sorry and apologised for his actions.

"No worries" I said

"Many a time my mouth and booze has nearly got me in the shit." I said

"Yeah, I know, but I didn't think they were Coppers!" he said.

"Lesson taught then, be very careful what you say and who you say it to". I continued.

A GUARDSMAN'S LOT

"Do you want a coffee you look like your suffering?" I said.

"Yes please Steve". He says

And that was the end of that.

One night Jan and I were at home in Twickenham after a good night out, and we went to bed. Then in the middle of the night there is a banging on my front door- BANG BANG BANG. I stuck my head out of the window and there is Tammy, motor bike and all in her black leathers! Shouting:

"Are you enjoying that fucking Geordie bitch?" she says

"You're going to be sorry you cunt how dare you!" she said

I called down, and told Tammy:

"To, Please shut the fuck up as people are trying to sleep"

Tammy was not budging, still standing there screaming abuse, it was like a scene from Fatal Attraction. She was round the fucking twist; I had to threaten her with the police. She left in a cloud of rubber; I must admit the Harley really did move. All we could do was have a laugh and go back to bed. I did phone Tammy the next day and explain the facts of life to her and told her that if she ever tries another stunt like that I would stick her Motor bike in her foul mouth. I never did hear any more from Tammy.

In the summer of 1988 I was sat outside a pub in Twickenham enjoying the warm summer evening, I thought I saw a face I recognised from the distant past entering the bar. I needed a refill and went inside to buy another pint. I was just about to order a pint of lager and a voice behind said,

"Well you old fucker aren't you going to buy and old mate one as well?" he said

Who was this guy? I knew the face but couldn't remember where from.

"Yes what will you have?" I said.

"Same as you Steve, please." He said

"Fuck" he even new my name. Heading back outside with the "face" following me, we

A GUARDSMAN'S LOT

sat down. From that moment on he didn't stop talking. He told me who he was and that he was now out of the game as he called it. It was a guy that was in the same platoon as me when I was a young Guardsman in Sharjah. For the sake of this part of the book I will call him Sid. I remember Sid, but only as a distant memory. He was a couple of years older than myself. In 1968 he had been a fitness freak and was always a bit of a loner. But the man sitting in front of me that night certainly didn't look like the man that I remembered. He was what I would describe as scruffy, ill-shaven and maybe down on his luck. After a bit of chit chat in which he described that he was now out of work had left the Army in 1987. Had been divorced and had three kids that didn't want any thing to do with him. I must admit I really felt sorry for Sid. He used to be one of the guys that was never late, always well turned out and really didn't make any waves. One thing about Sid was that he was really intelligent, too bright for the guards that's for sure. As the night moved on Sid asked me what I had been up to, so he got my sad saga of events.

"Well you know Steve you're not the only one that ever got shafted by this machine called the Army." He said

"Yeah, tell me about it", I said.

I had arranged to meet Jan for dinner that night we were going to meet at the Italian restaurant in Twickenham at nine. But with Sid and the drinks I didn't think I was going to make it.

"Excuse me Sid, I have to make a quick call" I said.

I went into the bar to call Jan, and cancelled our date. When I got back to the table Sid had got the beers in. He was what I would call a drink to get drunk guy, as opposed to a drink to enjoy guy, if that makes sense?

The drinking and conversation continued well into the night we even moved inside as the chill in the air was a bit too much for me

A GUARDSMAN'S LOT

to handle in my T-shirt. All the time I got the impression that Sid wanted to say something. I would talk about my tours in Ireland and he would start to say something and then clam up.

After we started on the whisky he did lighten up, and what he said made the hairs on my back stand up.

I will relay his story to you as he told me to best of my memory.

I don't know if it was true or not I will leave the decision up to you, the reader??.

<u>The story that Sid told.</u>

Sid had left the Battalion in Sharjah and went to try for the SAS.

He completed the selection course and did what the SAS do.

It was around this time that British intelligence was loosing the fight on obtaining information on the terrorists of the IRA. The

STEVE RUDGE

Government were scanning the ranks for people with certain qualities. The things they were looking for will be made clear as the story continues.

Sid found himself on a training course learning to talk with a Belfast Irish accent. On completion of the course all ties with England were severed, a new identification was given to him and he was let loose on the catholic community of Belfast in Northern Ireland. He took a job as a milk man in the local area, and he rented a room in a house in the Catholic area of Belfast. He told me that his landlady was a good fuck, with a cheeky grin on his face.

His tasking was to obtain information on a suspect terrorist and remove the threat. He didn't use the word 'assassinate', but I got the drift. I tried to ask him questions but it was like he was in his own little world. Sid continued, he didn't tell me how many he had removed but he did explain how it was done. His only contact with the real world was via some Colonel who would leave a (letter box) a designated drop point for notes, gun etc.

Sid would pick up the weapon, use it, and return it to the designated letter box.

"Steve", he said "here is a funny thing.

Friday was the day I used to collect the money for the milk, at the end of the shift. I was driving down the Falls road on the milk float and out popped three hooded guys all holding weapons, screaming for me to hand over the money for the cause.

"Here take it," he says.

When he got back to the yard he had to tell his boss that the money was gone.

All Sid was saying was.

The fucking paper work I had to fill-in was bloody stupid. I think he told me that he had been doing this work for about eighteen months, he told me that he was always wired and on edge but had to hide it otherwise he would have ended up being fed to the pigs.

The conversation got really deep and Sid seemed to drift off for a while, I thought it was the booze that was making him mellow. I looked at this man from the past and wondered what was going through his head.

He sat up straight and quick as a flash, he said:

"I fucked up. I missed my target."

"So what?" I said.

"NO. I MISSED MY TARGET" he said:

The tears were growing in his eyes!

"I missed my target and killed a little girl who ran in front of me just as I pulled the trigger, two in the head," Sid said.

He explained to me that all his training made him step over the poor kid and dispatch his proper target.

The next day they found Sid on his milk float staring into oblivion. He was extracted out of Belfast and put into a psychiatric hospital. He told me that after that he was regarded safe

A GUARDSMAN'S LOT

and they permitted him to leave and try and pick up his life again.

"HOW COULD I EVER BE THE SAME AGAIN" he said.

With tears running down his face. I sat in total silence for at least five minutes.

What this poor guy went through we will never understand.

Sid had composed himself, and as the barman was calling last orders.

"One for the road Sid?" I said.

"Yeah". "Please Steve." Said Sid.

I went to the bar and asked for two doubles, turned round to hand Sid his Whisky and he had left. I never saw Sid from that day to this.

"If you read this" "Sid", "good luck mate".

Jan and I were really settling down together well.

She took a job in the city, employed by a mate of mine, an American called Bill. I also set up a Company called "Alpha Omega", so in my spare time I used to make a few pounds carrying out investigations and minor security work. It was convenient for me, due to the fact that my office was co-located with Bill's, so Jan would take any calls for Alpha Omega if I was at Arborfeild.

The time came when I had to be shown off to Jan's folks. On the first available weekend we had off together, we planned the trip. Things were not good between Jan's parents and me. Billy had been the apple of Jan's Mum's eye, and I was seen as the big bad bastard.

Jan called her mum, and afterwards said to me, that we can visit, but mum says that we cannot share the bed.

"What!" I say.

Jan told her Mum that we would stay at the local hotel together.

"Don't worry" Jan said,

"I have squared it away; mum says we can sleep together" She said.

A GUARDSMAN'S LOT

So off we went to Hordon, County Durham. My first visit to Jan's mum and dad and I was like some school kid waiting for the cane.

It was a fucking disaster. I hadn't felt good all day, so that night we all went to the pub for a drink. Half way through my first pint, I had to rush to the toilet; I was puking my guts up and shitting through the eye of a needle.

I had to get out of there, I went back to the bar and told Jan, "that I had to go" so the whole family had to leave as well. I am trying really hard not to puke on the way back to the house. No such luck, all the way down the street, I am being as sick as a dog. Passer-by's must have thought I was a right piss cat drunk. Lord knows what the family thought of me. By the following day I felt fine. I had thoughts that Jan's Mum had tried to poison me!

Not really.

After lunch we set off back to London.

"Well that went well" I said to Jan.

No comment, from Jan.

The next weekend I collected Adam and Emma (my kids) from Grantham, and we took them to Richmond Ice rink. Adam being a little know it all, says:

Its OK dad I know what I am doing,

Then Adam fell flat on his arse. The kids had a good time, I think?

Jan showed Emma how to bake, and I was forced to eat blackened bits of pastry. Jan was really good with the kids and they got on like a house on fire.

My army work was ticking over and it was time for our annual reports. That's when the bosses write a report on their subordinates, it really didn't matter as I had all ready received a letter from Regimental Headquarters telling me, that no matter how many recommendations I received for promotion I will never get my Warrant Officer First Class.

If that were to be the case today, the regiment would find themselves on the wrong end of an industrial tribunal. I had already received two recommendations from the Depot. I looked at the report handed to me by the chief clerk of the College. It could not be me that the Commandant was talking about, this guy called Rudge was a super warrant officer etc, etc, etc, considering that I really didn't do much it was really impressive. Complete with my third recommendation for promotion.

I was still wheeling and dealing and I changed my car for a black Porsche 944. It went like shit off a shovel. Jan was the queen of the road, well not really, she wouldn't go over 40MPH as she was too scared to give it some, not surprising as She had only just passed her driving test.

Simon was one of the guys that I met at Porteuos camp when I was training the cadets. I invited him down for his birthday and took him out for dinner. Jan had been busy buying a load of little presents for him. A good night was had by all and Simon really enjoyed his presents, which consisted of one "Tommy The

Tank Engine" lunch box, a "two inch high wind up nodding penis" which Simon had great delight showing off his new toy and allowed the penis to nod all over the table.

Simon invited Jan and I to the Policeman's ball at Hendon. It was black tie with all the trimmings. So we had to go dress shopping for Jan, what a nightmare. She ended up looking like the bell of the ball in her purple taffeta evening dress, she looked gorgeous. The Ball was great, four bands in four different locations, three groups, and a couple of discos. We were like a dog with ten dicks not knowing where to go first. We left after the champagne breakfast which was laid on as well, took the taxi back to Simon's and slept for the whole of the day.

Thank you Simon, "it was a great night"

I was now moving into my last year of service. I handed over the Sergeants Mess Accounts to another guy, and was now back with B Company. Len was still there and making preparations to move to Zimbabwe, where he and his family intended to settle down.

I had decided that I was getting the hell out this country and I was making preparations with South Africa House to immigrate to South Africa. It was hard work convincing Jan to come with me, but finally she agreed. So both applications went in together. The wait would be a long one.

Part of leaving the army is a thing called resettlement training, this is to train you for civvy life, it could be taken in a number of ways, I spent my month of resettlement training at the office in London, teaching myself how to do more wheeling and dealing, it was money for jam.

In that month I also continued with the Freemasons, my big day was soon to arrive. I had studied hard and was soon to be up for my Master Mason. This is one of the big moments in a Mason's life. My Masters degree taken, it's all hands to the bar. I had gone from basic

STEVE RUDGE

Mason to Master in twelve months, which was a record.

One day when I arrived home from Arborfeild, Jan and the girl next door were at home. Jan was trying to see what was in the poor girl's eye. It looked really sore, 'so' I utilised my army medical training and put a huge patch over her eye having removed the offending eye lash.

We could not stop laughing, the patch was made out of gauze and sticky tape, and she looked like she had just had brain surgery. So much for my army medical training, she was fine the next day but never complained about any ailments again at our house.

Every summer the College would have a foot drill competition. Each of the Companies had to enter a team of thirty men, and the judges came from the Guards.

My Company had won last year, so we were looking for a clean sweep again, as this was to be my last one before I left the army.

A GUARDSMAN'S LOT

The lads worked really hard at mastering all the little tricks of the trade that I taught them.

Their drill kit had to be spotless, and hours of behind the scenes preparation was carried out, the whole Company helped out, cleaning boots, polishing brass buckles, pressing uniforms and a multitude of other things that needed doing.

Anyone could be marked down for even having his tie not flush to his collar. We were never told who the judges were going to be until the day of the Competition. B company drill team were ready to beat all comers.

The boys were good and knew it. All the other Company Sergeant Majors used to ask,

"Steve. How the fucking hell do you do it?"

"Simple" I would say,

"Tell the boys their good and they will be." I said

My boys march on to the parade ground we were the last on. They do their stuff. They were hot, really the best, but the accolades were not to be given to B Company, even though they were by far the best.

It would seem that my past would not go away. The chief judge of the day was a Grenadier RSM, who at one point in his miserable life was junior to me in rank. He was one of the ones that had ostracised me in Germany years before. This cunt had allowed his personnel dislike for me to influence his judgement, to hell with the thirty boys and their feelings, was I glad to be leaving soon. Even the Commandant was astounded by the results B Company were awarded, and we were awarded and rewarded by being placed last.

After the Competition, we are all expected to attend the Mess and tell the Judges how wonderful they are. I was not going to let this go without something said. I slide up to the Grenadier RSM the chief judge.

"How's your day going? Remember me?" I asked.

A GUARDSMAN'S LOT

"Yes, Company Sergeant Major, how are you?" He asked.

"Your very formal in my Mess, you can call me Steve if you like?" I suggested.

"No I don't do Christian names to junior warrant officers." He said.

"Fine," see you later." I say.

I was so angry. It was obvious from the start that he was being a right poppas prick. A formal lunch had been arranged for all the people involved in the drill competition. I remembered from the past that this prick could not hold his drink, and he knew he would be staying the night, so there was every chance he would lay one on and get pissed.

If I had anything to do with it he would be falling over in the next few hours. Just before lunch sat down I went into the kitchen and spoke to my mate the wine steward. The plan was hatched. During the five course lunch the waiters came and went, filling glasses, no one noticed that the bottle used to fill the glass of the Arsehole RSM was never used on anyone else's glass.

It wasn't long till the guy was slurring his words and getting louder. He was starting to make a prick of himself. There are always speeches to be given and that's always when the port comes out. So we didn't have much time to go with the wine, so the waiters were flying around with their bottles of wine. It got so blatant that the waiter serving the arsehole would say:

"Come on Sir, let me top you up." says the waiter

Dick head would swallow the glass and hold it out to be refilled.

By the time the port came round and the table was cleared, except for the cheese and port, he was out of his tree. The Commandant was starting to get a touch annoyed, as everyone was trying to talk over the very loud and very drunk prick of a chief judge.

A GUARDSMAN'S LOT

The chairman stands up and bangs on the table, the room goes quite, ready for the speeches.

The Chairman thanks all the Judges for coming to do a sterling job. Everyone claps hands and the Chairman sits down. He then bangs on the table and all is silent,

"I would now call on the chief judge to respond." The chairman said.

A big round of applause and the judge is trying to stand up, finally he gets up swaying on his feet. He is now swaying from side to side. What ever he was trying to say didn't sound like anything, it was the ramblings of a drunk.

The Commandant was scathing and nodded to the Chairman, who told the fool:

"Please sit down", said the chairman

"You" "are an embarrassment to yourself and your regiment". Said the chairman.

The whole luncheon party started to laugh and clap and the fool sat down or should I say fell into his seat. He had shown the Commandant just what a fool he was. One of the other judges was trying to distance himself from the fool.

"Mr Chairman" "I really must apologise for his behaviour". He said to Me.!!!!!!!

"You see" the college RSM was away and as the next senior it was my job to chair the lunch in his absence so "I was the chairman"." The deal I had setup with the wine steward was that the arsehole's bottles of wine would be lashed with vodka. We finished the port and left the table, with the arsehole still face down on the table, pissed out of his tree. I am convinced that the Commandant wrote to the RSM's Regimental Headquarters, to report the disgusting behaviour of one of its RSMs when invited to another unit. Bless him. I am sure his career took a nose dive from then on.

I drove home stone cold sober to Jan and laughed all the way home.

"Revenge as a meal is best served cold".

It was no conciliation for the boys that had worked so hard, but the story was leaked out, which put a smile on their faces. The commandant also spoke to me some time later in the month and the lunch was mentioned. I explained that the man must be a raging alcoholic, and that's probably why the battalion shipped him out to serve at some unknown outpost.

"Yes. I quite agree Sergeant Major," was the Commandant's response.

He walked off with a smile on his face. I believe that he had got news of the goings on at the lunch table. Never mind, he did have a good sense of poetic justice, and a good sense of humour.

I was now moving into my last six months of service. I handed over my Company to the new guy whom was to take my place. He was a Grenadier also, whom I had served with in Uganda. He was an OK sort of chap. The hand over took about a week, and I allowed him to do all the things that the Company Sergeant Major of B Company should be doing. I was also summoned to London to see the Regimental

Adjutant, Noddy. He was harmless and never did me any harm. Well, none that I was aware of. He went through the old patter how he was sorry to see me go. I said:

"Please let's cut this bullshit out."

He handed me a certificate of service and a 6 inch high bronze statue of a Grenadier dressed as per the eighteen hundreds.

"This is to say thank you and good luck for the future". He said:

It was just phoney.

"Thanks" I said.

Walking out of his office I dropped the statue in the bin.

"Bye." I said.

That was the last time I would ever have to deal with those bunch of cunts again.

I kept the certificate of service to remind me of the shit and stress that they had put me through.

"Well", not really, it had a nice frame.

A GUARDSMAN'S LOT

Back at Arborfeild it was my turn to start getting my Army kit ready for the very last time. I had to have a medical, to ensure that I was fit for discharge. I wonder which brave doctor would dare say I was not fit to leave.

I was declared A1 fit and so I could move on with the discharge procedures. When you leave the Army, you are handed a bit of paper that all departments have to sign, to indicate that you have nothing out-standing. This takes a few days to complete, and at the end of it you are left with your army socks and underwear, and that's about it. The rest is then re-issued if it's serviceable.

So, for the next few weeks I was wandering around in my civilian clothing. The Boys of B Company held a leaving party for me, which was held outside as the weather was still nice and warm. All the lads were wishing me well and the boss gave a little speech. It was all very nice. The Company had all chipped in and had presented me with a full size base drum converted into a beautiful coffee table. It took pride of place in my home.

For years I used to carry this hip flask with me when out in the field, it served me well at times when I was freezing my tits off. I must have had it for over eighteen years. I had the flask engraved and part of my goodbye speech was to present this to the Company.

The night was drawing to an end the lads were really sorry to see me go. I must admit I did get a small pang of regret. Well, only for a few seconds, as I then had to tip the boys back into their barrack rooms, as many of the lads really had too much to drink. But what the hell! I was the next best thing to a civvy.

I was still waiting for my authorisation to move to South Africa. I was on the phone every day to immigration department of South Africa House.

One of the provisos was that I had to have £30,000.00 on deposit and proof of the same. The South African immigration department

A GUARDSMAN'S LOT

needed to know that I would not be a drag on the South African economy. The money was no problem, I had made and saved my money, and was also going to get £22,000 from the army as part of my leaving settlement, complete with a monthly pension.

Due to exchange controls in South Africa I also sent money over to my bank in the States. I didn't want the South Africans to know too much. On my last visit to see Patrick in LA, I changed my account details, so that Patrick had authorisation to transfer funds from my US account to me when I was settled in South Africa. Big, big, big mistake. He helped himself to over $80,000 of my money. But that's another story.

Finally we got all the documents to get us to Africa, and we were advised that we should buy plenty of clothing from UK as the stuff in Africa was of poor quality. Jan and I took a couple of days off, and headed to Oxford Street, London.

STEVE RUDGE

Was I ever pissed off with shopping! On one of our shopping days I had arranged for all the Alpha Omega team, and any one else who had helped out, to join Jan and myself for dinner, at the Tower Hotel in London. Jan and I had been shopping all day. I had gone to the bank and withdrew a large amount of cash, as we would need a wad for other things. I gave the money to Jan to put in her hand bag. After a day's shopping we took a taxi to the Hotel, both looking like we had been on "Crackerjack", with bags and parcels loaded up to the gunnels. We jumped in the taxi, worn out, it's really tiring spending money. At the Hotel we unloaded all the shopping and went to the lounge to await our guests. Half way through our first cocktail, Jan jumps up.

"My bag!" She screams.

"What about it?" I said.

"It's in the taxi!" she said

A GUARDSMAN'S LOT

So now we are both in a flap, I am calling her all sorts of names, but in hindsight, bless her, it was understandable.

I went down to the hotel concierge and wanted to know if he saw the taxi licence number?

"No". "Sorry Sir", he said.

But we do have the number for the police who can call the taxis on the radio." He continued.

He went off and two minutes later returned to tell me that a call was being made.

We had just got back to the lounge, and I was requested to see the concierge, stood next to him was the taxi driver.

He was holding Jan's bag in his hand.

"I was on my way home and you were my last fare." He told me:

"I always check the cab before I knock off", "and found the bag on the floor. "I didn't look inside but brought it straight back here." The taxi man says.

"Thank you" I said.

I opened the bag and thank goodness the envelope was still there.

I pulled out a fifty pound note and gave it to him and thanked him for his honesty. Biggest tip ever, I would think.

Jan burst into tears. Bless her. It really was my fault, I should have checked.

Dinner was a great night we all got steaming drunk. I paid the bill, and Jan and I took a taxi home, this time the bag was strapped to Jan's wrist. We were also buying household items to take over to Africa; one of the items was a big two door fridge freezer. When it was delivered it wouldn't come through the doors in my little Twickenham house.

I told the delivery guys to put it in the garden by the back door. I covered it in plastic and had to leave it to weather the storms.

Once I had it plumbed in and set up in Africa it worked fine.

Back at Arborfeild I was requested to go and see the commandant for my final interview.

A GUARDSMAN'S LOT

There is a strange custom in the army when attending final interviews. You march in as a Sergeant Major, and then walk out as Mister. There I am in my suit and tie waiting to be marched in by the RSM. The Commandant pops his head round the door and tells me to just:

"Come in and sit down", says the Commandant

All very civilised I thought. I must have been in there about half an hour, he was telling me that I would be missed and that he knew who was running B Company and thanked me for my discretion.

He fully understood why I had such a hard time before and stated,

"It certainly would never have happened if you had been in my Regiment!" says the Commandant.

So that was my failing.

I had joined the wrong Regiment!

Wish I had known that, twenty five years ago, maybe my life would have been different.

But then this book would not have been written.

At the end of the little chat, the Commandant wished me well and it was sincere. We shook hands and I left. What a great guy. If ever we meet it will be my pleasure to buy him dinner.

That night the Mess members laid on a formal dinner night, "Dining Out," for me as my farewell, not only from the College but out of the Army. I was staggered by the number of mess members that came to say goodbye, I really didn't know I was so popular. "Gentlemen. I thank you all and I hope your careers were better than mine."

<u>Squad Halt.</u>
Finish.

PostScript.

After I had left Arborfeild I was on leave 'till my official discharge date of the 18th December 1990. Jan and I went to the States and got married. We visited Len in Zimbabwe, and then moved to South Africa, where we lived for nine years. My dealings in Africa were such that it might warrant another book.

I would like to thank the people that helped me in my career:

Jan- my lovely devoted crazy wife.

Andy Axten- for his friendship.

Susan- my ex-wife for giving me two beautiful children.

Simon- for playing so well with his penis at the dinner table.

Dave- for remembering a kindness.

Len- for giving me some good laughs.

I must include in this all the guys that I fail to remember, for which I apologise, but you know who you all are, thank you.

And to the ones who think, that they were above me, and who think that their shit doesn't stink. Well really it does!

Iraq, Miles. Thank you, buddy.

Directory of Abbreviations.

RSM: The Regimental Sergeant Major. The senior non commissioned officer in a Battalion, or the rank of warrant officer first class.

CSM: Company Sergeant Major, or Sergeant Major outside of the Guards. The senior warrant officer in a Company, but Junior to the RSM.

CQMS: In charge of the Company weapons and stores.

PAY SERGEANT: Same as the CQMS. Some times called "the pay bloke"

SLR: self loading rifle.

GPMG: General purpose machine gun.

Gobshite: Someone who acts like a total uncaring fool.

Grotty: Worse than dirty. Also a nickname.

Minging: Worse than Grotty.

Arse: Very foolish.

An arsehole: Someone who really needs taking out and shooting.

Adjutant: Captain/Major. Or see above.

RMP: Royal Military Police

Commandant: The Head Honjo.

NBC: Nuclear Biological and chemical.

Guardsman: Private Soldier in the Rest of the Army.

Lance Sergeant: Full Corporal in the Rest of the Army. He is permitted use the Mess.

Sergeants Mess: Place where Sergeants and above live/eat and get pissed (a private club and exclusive)

A Beasting: Getting punishment and made to use excessive physical energy to complete the task given. I.e.: running around like silly sods.

Blighty: Old word for Britain.

Bluffing: Trying to get out of work or a small lie.

MOD: Ministry Of Defence.

Crackerjack: 1960s television game, stacking peoples arms with all sorts of stuff.

MO: Medical Officer.

NAAFI: Place to get pissed or tea and snacks.

Zulu Warrior: Dancing like a prat and showing your arse. While singing.

NATO: The goodies: but unable to agree on any thing.

Warsaw Pact: The Baddies. One now owes Chelsea football club.

Arsehole: A complete and utter prat.

About the Author.

Steve Rudge was born in 1950, into a family who's Father was in the Royal Air force, Steve was not the most academic of the family.

Steve was wondering what he should be doing in the working world, and he wanted to join the Merchant Navy, his Mother dissuaded him on this. His Father wanted him to join the Royal Air Force, Steve being somewhat stubborn, went against all advice and went along to the local Army Recruiting Office, and promptly joined the Brigade Of Guards, so at the tender age of 15 in 1966 Steve was on route to be trained in one of the toughest Regiments in the British Army the "Grenadier Guards".

Lightning Source UK Ltd.
Milton Keynes UK
23 November 2010

163347UK00001B/5/A